When Storms Come

 **McMaster Divinity College Press**
Ministry Studies Series

VOL. 1   Thomas Edward Dow, *When Storms Come:*

A Christian Look at Job

When Storms Come
A Christian Look at Job

THOMAS EDWARD DOW

☙PICKWICK *Publications* • Eugene, Oregon

WHEN STORMS COME
A Christian Look at Job

McMaster Divinity College Press Ministry Studies Series 1

Copyright © 2010 Thomas Edward Dow. All rights reserved. Except for brief quotations in critical publications or reviews, no part of this book may be reproduced in any manner without prior written permission from the publisher. Write: Permissions, Wipf and Stock, 199 W. 8th Ave., Suite 3, Eugene, OR 97401.

McMaster Divinity College Press
1280 Main Street West
Hamilton, Ontario, Canada
L8S 4K1

Pickwick Publications
An Imprint of Wipf and Stock Publishers
199 W. 8th Ave., Suite 3
Eugene, OR 97401

Scripture references in the book, unless otherwise noted, are taken from the HOLY BIBLE, NEW INTERNATIONAL VERSION, Copyright © 1973, 1978, 1984 International Bible Society. Used by permission of Zondervan Bible Publishers.

www. wipfandstock.com

ISBN 13: 978-1-60899-276-8

Cataloging-in-Publication data:

Thomas Edward Dow.

When storms come : a Christian look at Job / Thomas Edward Dow.

viii + 146 p. ; 23 cm. Includes bibliographic references and index.

McMaster Divinity College Press Ministry Studies Series 1

ISBN 13: 978-1-60899-276-8

1. Bible. O.T. Job—Criticism, interpretation, etc. 2. Job (Biblical figure). 3. Suffering—Biblical teaching. I. Title. II. Series.

BS1415.2 D70 2010

Manufactured in the U.S.A.

Contents

Foreword • vii

Introduction • 1

1. Before the Storms: Job Introduced and Praised • 13
2. The Storms Break: God's Servant Tried and Trusted • 26
3. During the Storms: Reactions of Job—A Person Like Us • 38
4. During the Storms: Reactions of Job—The Person of Faith • 70
5. During the Storms: The Reactions of the Miserable Comforters • 92
6. The Storms End in a Storm: The Words of Elihu and the Word of the Lord to His Servant • 105
7. After the Storms: God's Servant Rewarded • 119

Conclusion • 124

Bibliography • 139
Modern Author Index • 141
Scripture Index • 142

Foreword

As we read through the Bible, we discover that there are certain books we enjoy while others leave us unsatisfied. This is true for great scholars and novices alike. For example, Martin Luther, that great leader of the Protestant Reformation, referred to the book of James as an epistle "full of straw." For years, I had been similarly unsatisfied with the book of Job. Though I read it at least once a year, it was always a chore. Possibly, as a result of personal losses, I felt too deeply the sorrow and suffering Job was forced to endure. Rushing through those 42 chapters, I found little to satisfy the longing in my soul. Like Job, I found it hard to see the light shine while the storms of life were raging around me.

Tom Dow's book, When Storms Come, reminded me of an experience I had a number of years ago. One night as I was driving home, I was caught in a blinding snowstorm. The weather was so bad that I could barely see the road; yet I was determined to get home. At one point I drove into a "white-out," where the blowing snow obscured my view. Now, not only could I not see what lay ahead, I could not even tell if I was on the road. In that desperate moment, I saw the faint light of a bright yellow gasoline station sign up ahead. I used that sign as a guide and headed for safety.

Similarly, When Storms Come did something I never thought possible. It opened the windows of heaven and let the light of God shine through the book of Job for me. This book does not trivialize human suffering or offer easy answers to hard questions, but faces the issue of suffering in the context of the existence and love of God. Throughout the book, Dr. Dow talks about the storms Job had to face and the questions with which he struggled. For Job, the storms, which were very real, were only made worse by the ramblings of his so-called friends. In the midst of all this, Tom Dow enables us to see the light the cross of Christ provides for those caught in life's storms.

This book should be read by every Christian, but especially by those who, like Job, are called upon to endure great suffering and loss.

—Rev. Jim Somerville,
Former President,
Compassion Canada

Introduction

How influential the book of Job has been on so many people and for so many reasons!

> Job stands far above its nearest competitors, in the coherence of its sustained treatment of the theme of human misery, in the scope of its many-sided examination of the problem, in the strength and clarity of its defiant moral monotheism, in the characterization of the protagonists, in the heights of its lyrical poetry, in its dramatic impact, and in the intellectual integrity with which it faces the "unintelligible burden" of human existence. In all this Job stands alone. Nothing we know before it provided a model, and nothing since, including its numerous imitations, has risen to the same heights. Comparison only serves to enhance the solitary greatness of the book of Job.[1]

So writes Francis Andersen in his fine commentary on Job.

Samuel Ballentine has recently published a marvelously detailed treatment of Job. As well as providing extensive exegesis and helpful sections of practical application, Ballentine brings together hundreds of literary and artistic illustrations that relate to the Joban text. Paintings and sculptures (photographed with commentary), passages from novels, poems, dramas and short stories, histories, biographies, and autobiographies, each of which relates somehow either to the whole theme of Job or to particular passages being discussed, are seamlessly woven into the text of the book. All of this illustrative material assists greatly in interpreting Job. It also serves to illustrate the geographical and cultural breadth of Job's timeless influence on human thinking.[2]

"Why do bad things happen to good people?" This problem, so profound, yet stated so simplistically in this oft-repeated question, has occupied the attention and absorbed the thinking of the ages. There are other versions of the question, of course. Why do people suffer? Why

1. Andersen, *Job*, 32.
2. Ballentine, *Job*.

suffering? Many people are still swayed by the philosopher's famous syllogism: If God is good and all-powerful there ought to be no evil in the world. There is evil; therefore either God is not omnipotent, or he is malevolent.[3] In the thinking of many people this leads to only one conclusion: faith in a God who is perfect in power and goodness is impossible. The only rationalistic road to travel is a mild form of skeptical agnosticism regarding both the nature of God and the explanation for the existence and prevalence of evil in the world. To the Bible-believing Christian, this conclusion is unacceptable, because the God revealed in Scripture is both all-powerful and completely good. Is there a way of understanding the existence of both God and evil in the world that upholds this view of God?[4]

God and evil—how can they coexist in creation? How is it that injustice and unrighteousness often seem so triumphant in a world created by an all-wise and all-powerful God of love and goodness? Why do people suffer who do not deserve suffering? How is the Christian, who takes the sovereignty of God so seriously, and who believes in God's absolute control over all things, to answer the critic who asks, "Can you reconcile your belief in the goodness of God and the multitudinous agonies of countless thousands of human beings on the face of the earth?"

The book of Job, believed by some to be the oldest book in the Bible, tells a story that touches on many of these concerns. It tells of a great and wealthy man stricken with incredible calamity. He is not just any man. Job is not Everyman.[5] He is God's servant, by God's own testimony the

---

3. Strahan, *The Book Of Job*, 2, quotes J. S. Mill's *Three Essays on Religion*, saying, "Logic states its clear, simple, and apparently irrefragable case: 'If the maker of the world can do all that he will, he wills misery, and there is no escape from the conclusion.'"

4. Any book that deals with human suffering must make reference to the work of Rabbi Harold Kushner, *When Bad Things Happen to Good People*. A quote will demonstrate his thesis and conclusion: "Laws of nature do not make exception for nice people. A bullet has no conscience, neither does a malignant tumour or an automobile gone out of control. That is why good people get sick and get hurt as much as anyone. No matter what stories we were taught about Daniel or Jonah in Sunday School, God does not interrupt the laws of nature to protect the righteous from harm ... Bad things happen to good people, and God does not cause it and cannot stop it" (p. 58). God, to Kushner, is loving and caring. But he is not yet able to completely control evil and chaos.

5. Some say Job is Everyman. Rohr, *Job and the Mystery of Suffering*, 36, says, "Is Job a historical character? It appears there existed an ancient legend of a pious man named Job ... Our anonymous author, five hundred years before Christ, took the old legend, perhaps an oral tradition, and expanded it to create a profound theology of the problem of evil, of conversion, growth and suffering. A good dramatist, the author brings in

best man of his time—the best morally and ethically, and the best piously and spiritually. Yet, godly and good man that he is, Job is stricken with a savage series of misfortunes that bring him to the brink of total despair.

The major portion of the book of Job is taken up with speeches in which Job and his counselors reflect upon and react to Job's chaotic dilemma. It would appear that these speeches raise almost all of the questions that can be conjured up in human thought regarding the issue of human suffering and its relation to divine justice and sovereignty. Satisfactory answers to all of these questions can hardly be expected to issue from a study of Job; but some answers to some questions will be the reward of the serious student of this magnificent poem.[6]

There are people who always read the end of a story before they read the beginning. The idea seems to be that if things turn out well, the story will probably make good reading. We will spend some time at the beginning of this study looking at material that appears near the end of Job—specifically Job's final speeches in which he autobiographically reflects on his life before the storm of trouble assailed him. These chapters, although adequately treated in many commentaries, are not discussed with reference to the character of Job as he really is to be initially understood, and thus some of their value is overlooked. Here, the end, or at least the near end of the story of Job, will be treated first, in an effort

---

various characters to question the protagonist or hero, in order to get us involved in the drama. Job is the symbol of the just Everyman, the good person, the person of faith." Wood, *Job and the Human Situation*, 41, states: "There is a strange air about the description of the friends' visit [in the Prologue]. In quite formal terms we are told how the friends made careful preparations to meet at some pre-arranged junction of their different routes. Then having met as planned, they complete the rest of the journey together towards Job's home. Like Job, these men are non-Israelite. Is the incidental reference to tribal affinities a further unconscious indication that the book is really about Everyman?"

6. Thomas Carlyle called the book of Job "one of the grandest things ever written with pen." Tennyson called it "the greatest poem of ancient or modern times" (Ellison, *From Tragedy to Triumph*, 13, 14). Commenting on the date of the book, Ellison says, "Young adopts the view of Delitsch that it was written in the time of Solomon, but the evidence can equally well be interpreted as supporting a later date. The simple fact is that nothing depends either on the date of composition or on the authorship. The suggestion that the book must be early because the law of Moses, the Exodus, etc., are not mentioned has no validity, because the characters in it are not Israelites, and it is no chance that in the speeches the name Jehovah is found only once (12:9) . . . The background is, in fact, kept deliberately as general and as vague as possible, so that the problem of Job may be seen in all its mystery, unobscured by any purely temporal considerations" (pp. 16, 17).

to take the man Job seriously and to find out just what kind of person it was who was subjected to such intense suffering. The attention given in the beginning of this study to Job's exemplary character, based as it was upon his commitment to honoring God, attempts to silence once and for all the repeated attempts that have been made to suggest that the trials inflicted upon Job were meant to improve his character and draw him closer to the Lord. Before his troubles Job was a godly and good man. The trials, I will suggest, came with the intent of driving the goodness and godliness out of him. That they failed is the supreme triumph of the book. Job remains Job from beginning to end. This decision to begin with an examination of Job's character rather than immediately giving attention to the Prologue that describes the source and nature of Job's calamities is one answer to the question, "Why another book about Job?"

The Prologue in chapters one and two is vitally important, however. I am writing from the conviction that the story of Job actually happened. It is not a mythical tale or a legendary allegory.[7] The prose sections at the beginning and end of the book, the Prologue and the Epilogue, are to be taken literally as history, and are not to be ignored or neglected when considering the poetical speeches of Job, his friends, and the Lord. With this in mind, the account of the dialogues in the Prologue between God and Satan (understood here as the devil—the serpent of Eden,

---

7. Many writers disagree, of course: e.g. Strahan, *The Book of Job*, 21: "The Prologue and Epilogue, which are in prose, contain in outline an epic tale of fallen greatness, which the poet uses as the dramatists of Greece used the ancient legends of their country. Based on this story of primeval sorrows, the poem is in the deepest sense real and true, though the reader is not meant to take either the epic or the dramatic part of it as historical fact." Conservative thinkers have always had trouble understanding how something can be "in the deepest sense real and true," while at the same time being historically false. The integrity and historicity of Job are defended by Archer, *Survey of Old Testament Introduction*, 459, 463. Archer seems to agree with Delitsch, whom he describes as suggesting, "that the book was not meant to be a historically accurate transcript of words actually spoken in the patriarchal period, but that it was probably intended as a drama for which the dialogue had been composed by the author . . . Delitsch contends that no Hebrew reader would have understood the speeches in Job as a verbatim report, since the narrative was put into a poetic, dramatic form. Yet even as drama, Job is not to be dismissed as mere fiction, for the author may well have composed it under the inspiration of the Holy Spirit and accurately represented the sentiments and theological opinions historically expressed by the parties concerned. It was simply that the dramatic or poetic form in which they were composed was the product of the literary artist. If, then, the book did not purport really to be a reporter's transcript and would not have been so understood by the ancient reader, it should be understood and interpreted by the modern reader in the light of the author's original intention."

the tempter of Christ, the evil one of the Lord's Prayer), and the trial of Job occasioned by those dialogues, will be given serious attention and analysis.[8]

Many of Job's questions asked in the poetical section of the book are based upon his ignorance of the contest set up between God and Satan in the Prologue. We know from the Prologue that Satan is the one who brought severe trouble into Job's life. Job is convinced, however, that God is the sole author of his misfortunes. This he finds unbearable, unable to accept the view that God, whom he had hitherto known to be good and kind, is for some unfathomable reason now treating him unfairly, unjustly and with mysterious malignity. Ultimately he comes to the conclusion that he is not going to get a satisfactory answer to this dilemma immediately, but he determines to believe in God's ultimate goodness, fairness, and justice in spite of appearances to the contrary. He is convinced that if he maintains faith and integrity he (and God) will be vindicated sooner or later even if he has to endure unintelligible suffering to the point of death. God finally speaks powerfully to him, and Job is abundantly satisfied with God's words. As far as we know, Job never learns about the issues described in the Prologue. This may lead

---

8. Commenting on whether the prose and poetry sections were originally part of the same work, Harrison, *Introduction to the Old Testament,* 1037, states, "However, not all those scholars who separate the prose prologue and epilogue from the rest of the book are aware that there is no objective evidence whatever for the suggestion that the prose sections were added at a later period to the poems by an anonymous redactor. Alleged evidences of discrepancy between prose and poetic passages are often quite unconvincing." The section entitled "Critical Problems Connected with Job," pp. 1031–42, is very helpful. And note Fyall, *My Eyes Have Seen You,"* 19, who writes, "There are a number of reasons for seeing these [Prologue, Epilogue and poetic sections] as the product of one mind." Andersen, *Job,* 55, gives a conclusion with regard to the unity of Job that deserves quotation: "At this distance in time the details of the complex process of literary growth and subsequent transmission of Job will never be known. Arguments for the disunity of the book are not conclusive, and in spite of numerous difficulties, the Hebrew text is probably in pretty good shape. It is possible that the whole work is the product of a single mind, and insoluble textual problems need not prevent us from making sense of the book as a whole." Andersen's treatment of introductory issues with regard to Job seems judicious, fair and balanced (*Job,* 15–73). Worth careful reading is Andersen's excellent discussion entitled, "The Problems of Suffering in the Book of Job," pp. 64–73. Regarding Job's uniqueness vis à vis Job-like stories in Ancient Near Eastern literature, Andersen summarizes the latter, and concludes, "The literature of the Ancient Near East has not yielded another Job. There is a considerable list of writings from this region . . . which remind one of Job in this way or that. But none comes close to Job when each work is examined as a whole. Each shows more differences than similarities" (p. 31).

the reader to conclude that the Prologue really is of small import when discussing the meaning and value of the book of Job. But the reader of Job, and all who suffer undeservingly, will, I believe, profit from reflecting seriously on these matters contained in the Prologue that touch upon the source of human trials and how they are to be understood in the light of an understanding of the character of God.

The Prologue makes much of Satan and his challenge to God regarding Job's integrity. It is Satan who inflicts Job so severely. Satan is not mentioned in the book of Job beyond chapter two, but it seems to me that his destructive works in Job's life are the very issues of the poetic sections. "Who has done this to me?" Job asks, (he seems to know nothing of the being or character of Satan), and if God did it, what am I to make of his character in respect to me as his loyal servant? So, although Satan is absent and silent for the remainder of the book, the results of his destructive activity and the questions arising from this with regard to God, evil, and suffering form the core of the Joban story. This is why so much attention is given to Satan in the pages below.

Some years ago, I stood in a funeral home with parents of a child tragically killed in a sledding accident. Was I there as God's ambassador to convince them that a good God willed this awful event? As I listened to the voice speaking to my mind, I heard distinctly Jesus' word from the parable of the wheat and the weeds, "an enemy did this . . . the enemy who sows [the weeds] is the devil" (Matt 13:28, 39). Oftentimes (as repeatedly in the book by Job's friends), God is unfairly blamed for catastrophes and in the process loses the credibility and respect he deserves. Of course Satan is not omnipotent; he is not God's equal in any way. But the Bible teaches (and the book of Job asserts) that he possesses malevolent power, and that he employs it harmfully. He is the First Cause behind all secondary causes that bring misery into the human situation. He is indeed the Enemy.

We live in a fallen world; the Devil was the catalyst who tempted our first parents to deny God's truthfulness and disobey his command. They (and, consequently, we and the whole of humanity) are responsible for sinful choices with disastrous consequences. But Satan shares the guilt for the world's woes. When he is at work, it is wise to discern his presence and activity, and follow Job's example in remaining faithful to God as we endure whatever it is that evil and the Evil One have brought our way. So I will attempt to give Satan his due in this book. Sorrow and tragedy are part of the legacy of the Fall. Good people, godly people, suffer along with the rest of the race. Behind much of this misery is The Enemy.

Job was a very human sufferer. He complained (often bitterly), questioned and argued with his friends and with God about the meaning of all that was happening to him. Several sections of this study will be taken up with analyzing Job's very human reactions to suffering. Along with sympathizing deeply with this sufferer, this analysis will take the liberty of dialoguing with Job as he reacts to the suffering through which he is passing. Readers can do this in their role as observers of the whole story, since they know of the celestial discussions of the Prologue, of which Job was ignorant, and they witness the outcome of the story as Job's faith prevails. As well, Job lived long before Christ, and as believers in Jesus we may and will dare to bring insights from the New Testament into our interaction with Job the human questioner.

But Job was also and above all a God-fearing believer. A good number of his reactions are faith-inspired and hope-filled. These reactions will be discussed as well, and there will be times when sheer admiration for this suffering saint will be very evident.

Job's three friends had much to say about his suffering and their opinions of it and of him. Their conduct as described in the Prologue, and their words of counsel contained in the speeches, are extremely instructive to anyone who is involved in ministering to people who are in trouble. What they did and said, and did not say, provide the reader with a handbook of illustrative material concerning the reactions of observers to the dilemma of God's servant in suffering. Their reactions will be discussed in some detail, as will the contributions made by the mysterious interjector, Elihu.

Strange as it may sound, the major figure of the book of Job is not Job; it is God, who is in a very real sense on trial in this story. The great questions of existence and meaning, and particularly those that involve the mysteries of suffering and tribulation, are always and inevitably addressed to the Almighty. It is God's justice, his veracity, his worthiness to merit people's trust and confidence that are the issues of Job. Much attention in the following pages must and will be given to God's character and to God's words, especially those he speaks immediately prior to the end of the book of Job.

The end of the story of Job is, of course, the story of faith triumphant and faith rewarded for Job. This man of great endurance and patience is once again restored to his position of wealth and respect. He lives on to a ripe old age, again blessed with children, lands, and the smile of God. He dies a very old man, contented, lamented, and satisfied. Our study must grapple with the issue of credibility at this point. Is it conceivable that Job could, in the end, be so blessed? Is it right to think that faithful believers who endure much suffering will be rewarded so magnanimously? Again, we reflect on Jesus' words to sufferers, "Blessed are you... for great is your reward in heaven."

Why another book about Job? There are several extant views of suffering and the Christian reaction to it, which, I believe, indicate the need for another look at Job and his predicament. For several years there has been teaching abroad that suggests that the believer should thank God for all that transpires in life—the sufferings as well as the successes. Christians have been urged to give thanks for troubles, and to see them all as heaven-sent pedagogues whose mission is to make better people of us. There is certainly a measure of truth in this philosophy, ("count it all joy," "In everything give thanks") but, when carried to the extreme, it suggests that there is no room in the Christian's emotional life for questioning the origin of troublesome experiences, much less for weeping over them and desiring above everything else their departure. Trials are to be welcomed and celebrated is the essence of this thinking. But a careful study of Job will defend the validity and viability of expressing genuine sorrow and agony when storms come, agony that a believer can, and to be human, should, experience, without the burden of guilt. In the Authorized Version of Jas 5:11, Job is described as having "patience." "The patience of Job" suggests that he suffered without complaining or murmuring and that this is how we should suffer too. The word is better translated, however, as in the NIV, as "perseverance." Job's blatant impatience in his speeches is human and understandable. He did, however, persevere and endure to the end, was vindicated by God, and restored.

In a way, the book of Job is a "sometimes" book, needed as a corrective to some "always" concepts. Sometimes trials are not sent by God to punish wickedness or to teach life lessons. Sometimes troubles are not the chastening hand of a loving Father nudging believers back to obedience, but come as potential faith-destroyers from the Enemy's hand. Sometimes God allows his servants to be tested (sometimes, apparently, even by Satan!), with great agonies, God all the while trusting them to remain faithful no matter what life or the powers of evil may inflict upon them. Sometimes God allows his servants to pass through hard times to prove to all beings natural and supernatural that believers are not exempt from the human troubles and sorrows that are humanity's lot in this fallen world, and that faith, when tested severely, can survive, even when God seems deaf and invisible. Sometimes God remains silent and hidden as the believer faces the dark night of the soul seemingly alone, with only the memories of better times with God and the determined confidence that faith and faithfulness must be maintained no matter what. Sometimes persevering faithfulness is rewarded in this life; Job eventually experienced this. Other portions of Scripture (e.g., Heb 11:35–40) indicate that for many, rewards will have to wait until the life to come. But come they will. Sometimes, perhaps quite unknowingly, endurance on the part of his servant can even make God proud, as Job certainly did.

Hopefully, a patient examination of this ancient piece of wisdom literature will also help dispel the errors that reside at the heart of all prosperity theologies. Some extreme prosperity teachers make no room for suffering or loss in the Christian's experience. All Christians, it is claimed, have the right to be healthy and prosperous all the time. If they are not, there is a lack of understanding of their full rights as believers. Such teachers maintain that physical, emotional, and even financial healing have been secured for believers through the atonement. To misunderstand this truth and not appropriate these blood-bought blessings by faith, they say, is to live below our privileges as men and women of God. Far from being causes for celebration, life's storms are to be expelled, driven out, and exorcised. They have no place in the life of God's child. The book of Job stands as a corrective to all these notions. Sometimes God allows the best of his servants to suffer in every conceivable way and sometimes for a long time.

Of course I know that God is able to heal the sick, and I know of many instances where this has been the case. And there seems to be no biblical warrant for believing that poverty and want are virtuous; the promise is that our needs will be met. Job in the beginning (and at the end of the story!), is a wealthy, nonetheless godly, man. As well, it is clear that there are Scriptures, (e.g. many verses in Proverbs), that posit a connection between righteousness and financial security. But there are other Scriptures to balance these ideas. People who live by faith are not always rewarded in this life with prosperity and abounding health, and into the lives of the godliest, sufferings of the most intense sort may come. Like the teaching of those mentioned above who call for rejoicing in adversity, it is the "always-ness" of these theologies that calls for correction. Believers cannot always claim perfect healing or always claim financial success. We do not always reap what we sow in this life. Job is a book that helps to keep these ideas in balance. Bad things do happen to good people; obviously bad things happen to all people in this life "under the sun." The question is not so much why these things happen; we may not know or need to know why, though we can have an understanding of where they come from. The question of prime importance is, how will the man or woman of faith react and respond when such periods of stress come? Is faith a valuable resource in aiding the believer in wholesome coping, sometimes a way *through* agonizing trials rather than merely a way out of them? Is it the way of wisdom (Job is part of ancient wisdom literature after all), to hang on to God and virtue no matter what circumstances might come? The story of Job answers affirmatively.

How did this book come to be written? Certainly it came about from personal experiences through which I have passed, during which deep convictions have been formulated. These convictions are deemed to be worth sharing because they might help someone else. In the early stages of writing a previous form of this book, my beloved first wife, Carolyn, was diagnosed with breast cancer, and after much suffering, which lasted the better part of ten years, she passed away. I have written details of this experience as part of the Conclusion of this book. Job helped me deal with the incredible anguish I suffered, and this experience has strengthened my desire to share insights gained through my grief and my study of Job.

Inspiration has also come from others, not the least of whom were students of Emmanuel Bible College in Kitchener, Ontario, where it has been my privilege to teach for over forty years. My field of interest and my formal education have largely been in History and this I taught at various levels for many years. In a small institution at a certain stage of its academic development, however, one was asked to do things that might not present themselves as opportunities in larger, more intellectually mature schools. One semester I was asked to teach a course entitled "The Poetry of the Old Testament." I was not very enthusiastic about it at the time, but I had little choice, and so began my love affair with biblical poetry and wisdom. Job was part of the course, and as I read and reread this ancient classic, I became more and more convinced that there were truths to be gleaned in it that were nothing short of remarkable. I have taught the course many times since. This book in part evolved out of those teaching sessions.

The book of Job deals with issues that are incredibly timely—or timeless: suffering, death, tragedy, loss, and God and a servant of God in the midst of it all. Seeing the effect of teaching this book to generations of students, and being taught by them in the process, became a major reason for my conviction that I had to write down these thoughts in the hope that readers will be aided by insights from Job, both the ideas that other authors have suggested and some personal insights I have seen clearly explained nowhere else.

In addition, my interest in the subjects treated in Job developed through many years as a pastor. I have spent countless hours in hospitals and funeral homes, at gravesides, and at the bedsides of scores of people in distress. I have counseled those who were facing storms of all kinds and have come to the conviction that the most important coping tool one can have is faith and confidence in an all-wise, all-powerful, and all-loving God. Job has been a great resource for me in pastoral ministry. Every pastor will profit from familiarity with Job.

This book is not intended to be a scholarly treatise. It is written for pastors, lay counselors, college students, as well as for people passing through the storms of life and for people who desire to minister to them. The footnotes do make reference to several recent and not-so-recent Job studies with the hope that these will assist in engaging with the biblical text of Job, but many scholarly issues are simply not addressed here at all. The reader will note that several references are made to the work of James Strahan, who wrote in 1914. This old friend has been in my library for many years, and has become a favorite, written as it is in elegant early twentieth-century style. Strahan's interpretations reflect his theology of early modernism, and I use him often as an example of arguments with which I disagree, as well as for sentiments with which I do agree and which he expresses with much more erudition and grace than I do.

So we move to our discussion of the book of Job itself. Please forgive the faults of my small book. What is valuable, take and use to the glory of God. The rest discard. This book is meant for everyone, for we all live in the same world as Job, and his story can help us all immensely if we will just take it seriously.

1

Before the Storms: Job Introduced and Praised

JOB INTRODUCED AS A MAN WHO PLEASED GOD

WE NATURALLY WANT TO know something of the man Job—what can we say about him? Are there any clues to his personality and character? Of course we know what the author of the book thought of him: "In the land of Uz there lived a man whose name was Job. This man was blameless and upright; he feared God and shunned evil" (Job 1:1). We know, too, what the Lord said about him: "My servant—there is no one on earth like him; he is blameless and upright, a man who fears God and shuns evil" (Job 1:8). It seems as though God wanted to praise his servant to Satan; it was the Lord who initiated the conversation about Job. God spoke in glowing terms of his man. "See, there is my servant. See what a man he is! A good man, and a godly man! Behold, my servant!" God was pleased with Job. God praised his servant. We might even say that God bragged about his man. Mason comments:

> This verse leaves no doubt that Job really was a "blameless and upright" man and that such was not simply the subjective opinion of the book's author. Job's righteousness was a divinely attested fact, and from the very beginning it is the Lord Himself—not Job or any other human being—who sets out to justify this man and to establish his innocence. Moreover, this is not a defensive reaction on the Lord's part, but an offensive initiative. It is the Lord who issues the first challenge, the first taunt, by aggressively boasting to Satan about Job. Thus the unimpeachable righteousness of Job is the very core of the book, the linchpin upon which the entire plot hangs. God's praise for His servant is so open and lavish, and His backing so unqualified, that if at any point in the

ensuing struggle we are tempted to question the integrity of Job's faith (as his friends do, relentlessly), it will not really be Job we are questioning, but the Lord.[1]

When we stop to think about it, it is rather amazing that we have a book in the Bible that begins with God praising a human being. After all, the Bible is a book that directs mortals to praise the Lord, and the pages of Scripture contain the doctrine of the sinfulness and depravity of humanity. The dignity of the human person is a dogma that the evangelical wing of Christianity has shied away from, and rightly so in proportion to the extent to which that view has softened the concept of the lostness of people and the necessity of divine grace in human redemption. Nevertheless, it needs to be pointed out that there are examples in the Scriptures of people with whom the Lord was pleased. Daniel was called "greatly beloved," David was "a man after God's own heart," and God praised Job.

JOB'S CHARACTER REVEALED IN THE WORDS OF GOD

The idea that God can be pleased with a mere human, that a person's godly goodness can bring delight to the heart of the Heavenly Father, need not be foreign to us. We may be true to our belief in original sin and to our conviction that the Scriptures teach no doctrine of sinless perfection and still pray, "Lord, help me to follow Job's example. Help me to live by your grace as your servant so that you may be proud of me. Be pleased with my heart's love for you. Be pleased with my life of service. May the mission statement of my life be that of the Lord Jesus himself, 'I always do that which pleases him' (John 8:29). And may there be times when I hear the echo of those words uttered at Jesus' baptism, 'This is my beloved son in whom I am well pleased.'"

It might be noted at this point that Job is described as being "the richest man in the east." Can a rich man please the Lord? Apparently the answer is yes, if the story of Job is to be believed. We will see how Job used his wealth in unselfish ways as we explore later chapters in which he describes his character for us. It is enough here to note that God was pleased with Job, not in spite of his wealth or because of his wealth, but because of the kind of man he was. In the story of the rich young ruler, Jesus said to his disciples, "How hard it is for a rich man to enter the king-

---

1. Mason, *Gospel according to Job*, 29.

dom of heaven!" In fact, Jesus said it would be easier for a camel to go through the eye of a needle than for a rich person to get into heaven. The puzzled disciples asked, "Who then can be saved?" And Jesus' famous answer followed: "With man this is impossible. But with God all things are possible" (Matt 19:24–25). It is possible for rich people to get to heaven. It is possible for rich people—as in Job's case very rich people—to live lives that are pleasing in the sight of God. There are those who believe possessions can only be hindrances to a true understanding of God, and they must be abandoned or taken away, their possessor stripped to the point of utter need if real relationship with the divine is to be achieved.[2] The book of Job says that this is not necessarily the case.

JOB'S CHARACTER REVEALED BY HIS LIFESTYLE

Other than what is supplied to us in these testimonials, does the book offer any additional information about Job's character? Yes, for first we have the account in the first chapter of his concern as a father and as a priest of his home. He cared for his family and prayed regularly and earnestly for his children and for their spiritual welfare.

---

2. Rohr, *Job and the Mystery of Suffering*, seems to believe that Job needed to be stripped of possessions and standing in order to hear from God. "God can set us right only by breaking us down. As long as we remain in a self-assured, righteous, left-brain position . . . there is no way we can be bridge builders or reconcilers. We are going to see in Job how God breaks this man down so he can enter into a newer and better definition of truth, a better understanding of how God creates life on earth" (p. 44). So Rohr's point seems to be that the storms are sent by God to reduce Job to what he calls "pure desire." "Job has been simplified by suffering, which is what suffering always does. He is reduced to pure desire" (p. 123). Yet Rohr has said previously, "Job is defined as a good and just man. It seems fair to say that this saga does not create Job's faith; rather it identifies it and names it. His troubles don't make Job into a saint. They confirm the goodness already there" (p. 32). There seems to be some contradiction in these thoughts. Rohr's thesis throughout is that poverty is the truest road to sainthood: "Every real saint eventually left the system of possessions, privilege and power, so that he or she could hear and speak the truth. In doing so, they were joining Jonah in the whale, Jeremiah in the cistern, Job on the dunghill, and Jesus on the cross. It seems to be the way" (p. 104). When he comments on Job's autobiography in Job 29, Rohr says, "There's a bit of pride still there in spite of everything and his self righteousness is still growing." It seems that in spite of their best efforts, many authors cannot resist finding fault with Job, fault which is being stripped from him by suffering. It is this tendency I am arguing against throughout *When Storms Come*. If Job really found the truth of God only by surrendering possessions, power, and health, how can his restoration to all of this be reconciled? Rohr's Franciscanism colors his analysis constantly.

> His sons used to take turns holding feasts in their homes, and they would invite their three sisters to eat and drink with them. When a period of feasting had run its course, Job would send and have them purified. Early in the morning he would sacrifice a burnt offering for each of them, thinking, "Perhaps my children have sinned and cursed God in their hearts." This was Job's regular custom. (Job 1:4–5)

Job sets a fine example of faithful, prayerful, concerned parenthood, having established, as a regular custom, a definite time of prayer and intercession for his children. What an inspiration for us who are parents to be intercessors for our loved ones!

JOB'S CHARACTER REVEALED IN THE WORDS OF HIS FRIENDS

Then, too, we have the commendation of his friends. In the fourth chapter, before the severe criticisms directed against his friend begin, Eliphaz speaks of Job's ability to counsel and to bring encouragement to those who needed it. Job's words were powerful in lifting up feeble hands and weak knees! "Think how you have instructed many, how you have strengthened feeble hands. Your words have supported those who stumbled; you have strengthened faltering knees" (Job 4:3–4).

We may be tempted to believe that "words are cheap," and that what we have to say to people, especially suffering people, is of little practical value. Children are taught to respond to verbal abuse by repeating the adage, "Sticks and stones may break my bones, but names will never hurt me." Not so. Words have a great deal of power—they can be very effective weapons or very useful construction tools. Verbal abuse may be as painful and as damaging as physical abuse. Words may wound, cut, and damage those who receive them. The scars from a word beating can last a long time! On the other hand, words can soothe, comfort, heal, and minister great refreshment. This is speech therapy of a different sort, but genuine therapy nevertheless.

Job used his tongue to bless people; his words acted as a buttress and support for people who might otherwise have stumbled had he not spoken to them. Considering Job's example, we take to heart the words of Frances Ridley Havergal, "Take my voice and let me sing always, only for my King; take my lips and let them be filled with messages from Thee."

JOB'S CHARACTER REVEALED IN HIS OWN WORDS: CHAPTER 29—READING THE END OF THE STORY FIRST

If we read on late in the book, we discover more information about Job, and this information comes to us from the man himself. In chapters 29 and 31 especially, Job becomes very personal in his discussion with his friends and with the Lord. He talks about himself and he talks about his character. "This is the kind of man I have been," he says in these passages. "If you want to know what kind of person I am, I will tell you." And he does tell us.

In chapter 29 Job is longingly looking back upon his life before all the troubles befell him. We might entitle the passage, "Oh, for the good old days!" Listen to his sad plea for a happier time, and observe the character of the man revealed in it. Job has lost everything—family, possessions, honor, reputation; even his health has suffered severe deterioration. Seated in deep grief upon the ash heap of suffering, he speaks bravely in his own defense.

> How I long for the months gone by, for the days when God watched over me, when his lamp shone upon my head and by his light I walked through darkness! Oh, for the days when I was in my prime, when God's intimate friendship blessed my house, when the Almighty was still with me, and my children were around me, when my path was drenched with cream, and the rock poured out for me streams of olive oil. (Job 29:2–6)

The first and most important thing Job remembers and longs for is the friendship of the Lord. The lamp of the Lord shining on his head, the light of the Lord leading through the darkness, the intimate friendship of the Lord blessing him and his family—these things meant more to Job than anything else, and he longed fervently for their return. In his golden days, Job was first and foremost a man who walked with God.

Listen to Job as he tells in this chapter of the honor and respect he used to have, because of the large-hearted man he was, and still claims to be:

> When I went to the gate of the city and took my seat in the public square, the young men saw me and stepped aside and the old men rose to their feet. The chief men refrained from speaking and covered their mouths with their hands; the voices of the nobles were hushed, and their tongues stuck to the roof of their mouths. Whoever heard me spoke well of me, and those who saw

> me commended me, because I rescued the poor who cried for help and the fatherless who had none to assist him. The man who was dying blessed me; I made the widow's heart sing. I put on righteousness as my clothing; justice was my robe and my turban. I was eyes to the blind and feet to the lame. I was a father to the needy; I took up the case of the stranger. I broke the fangs of the wicked and snatched the victims from their teeth. (Job 29:7–17)

The picture that comes through in these verses is that of a man who is just, kind and genuinely good-hearted, not afraid to get involved in someone else's troubles, if he felt that person was being wronged and he could use his influence to defend the wronged one and drive off the wrongdoer.

The autobiographical material in chapter 31 adds even more to our understanding and appreciation of Job. Each verse in this chapter deserves to be studied carefully. Here is revealed a man of purity, honesty, equity, fairness, and compassion. Job is a man who was unselfish, considerate, generous, hospitable, and loyal to family and friends. Above all, he was a godly man, living his life in the realization of the existence and omnipresence of Almighty God, before whom he lived, and to whom he was answerable.

> I made a covenant with my eyes not to look lustfully at a girl. For what is man's lot from God above, his heritage from the Almighty on high? Is it not ruin for the wicked, disaster for those who do wrong? Does he not see my ways and count my every step? (Job 31:1–4)

Job professes to be a man of inward *purity*. He has not been guilty of lust. The mention of a girl suggests a reference to his early life, before marriage. Job deliberately determined, like Daniel, not to defile himself. His rationale was the fact of God's omnipresence. God's eye was upon him; to consider fornication would be to sin before God's very eyes, and this would be to court disaster and judgment. The ethics of this good man derive from his absolute assurance of the existence and all-seeing presence of the Righteous God.

> If I have walked in falsehood or my foot has hurried after deceit—let God weigh me in honest scales and he will know that I am blameless. (Job 31:5–6)

Before the Storms: Job Introduced and Praised

Job professes to be a man of inward truthfulness. He speaks of not walking in falsehood, as though honesty and veracity are his daily habit as he passes through life. Double-tongued deceit has never been his practice; Job indicates that it has been his lifestyle to be sincere and transparent, and he calls on God, who knows the heart, to witness his truthfulness.

> If my steps have turned from the path, if my heart has been led by my eyes, or if my hands have been defiled, then may others eat what I have sown, and may my crops be uprooted. (Job 31:7–8)

Job asserts his *honesty*; he has not strayed from the path of righteousness. His heart has not been led astray by the lust of his eyes.

> If my heart has been enticed by a woman, or if I have lurked at my neighbor's door, then may my wife grind another man's grain, and may other men sleep with her. For that would have been shameful, a sin to be judged. It is a fire that burns to Destruction; it would have uprooted my harvest. (Job 31:9–12)

Earlier he had claimed to be innocent of fornication. Here Job gives his opinion of adultery, and insists that he has been faithful to his wife, avoiding the opportunities that must have come to a man of his stature to engage in extra-marital sexual relationships.

In our day, sexual sins are all too prevalent in the world and broken marriages due to adultery are becoming common even among professing Christians. Almost weekly we hear of another marriage on the rocks—and too many of them involve those engaged in active ministry. Consider the resolve of this ancient patriarch who realized that the road of adultery is the road to destruction. Though he lived hundreds of years before Christ, Job had a moral sense sadly lacking among many today. Adultery to Job would be shameful, a "sin to be judged." One can almost sense his blush at the mere thought of being unfaithful, and his searing anger regarding this sin against the marriage vow. To my wife, to my vows, to my God, to my own sense of right behavior—I have been *loyal*, declares Job.

> If I have denied justice to my menservants and maidservants when they had a grievance against me, what will I do when God confronts me? What will I answer when called to account? Did not he who made me in the womb make them? Did not the same one form us both within our mothers? (Job 31:13–15)

Here Job states his attitude towards those who have been in his employ. He has been just and fair with them, he claims. He has treated them with *equity*, without prejudice, and the reason for his behavior is remarkable.

Job is convinced that God is the Father of all human beings, rich and poor alike. If God is Father, then in a real sense all human beings are equal members of his family. Men and women cannot be treated as chattel, as livestock, as slaves, as tools, or as implements. People must be treated as persons, Job insists, because God made us all. Before him we stand. To him we are answerable for the way we treat our fellow human beings. This notion of looking upon people not as things to be used but persons to be respected seems very modern to present-day readers. But the idea is as old as Job, as old as the sudden realization that comes to a person who really takes the existence, the personality, and the reverence of God seriously: Whom God has created, I must for his sake respect, honor, and treat with humane kindness and justice.

The apostle Peter had a hard time with this concept, and had to be traumatically convinced of its truth (Acts 10:15), "Do not call anything impure that God has made clean," God told him. This is a text that many in the world, warped by race pride, face pride, or place pride, need to ponder very seriously. The modern reader can only be surprised and impressed to find Job in possession of so valuable and meaningful a view of what it means to be a human being before God.

> If I have denied the desires of the poor or let the eyes of the widow grow weary, if I have kept my bread to myself, not sharing it with the fatherless—but from my youth I reared him as would a father, and from my birth I guided the widow—if I have seen anyone perishing for lack of clothing, or a needy man without a garment, and his heart did not bless me for warming him with the fleece from my sheep, if I have raised my hand against the fatherless, knowing that I had influence in court, then let my arm fall from the shoulder, let it be broken off at the joint. For I dreaded destruction from God, and for fear of his splendor I could not do such things. (Job 31:16–23)

Liberality, kindness, justice, and generosity—all of these qualities shine through in Job's noble words. An unselfish, sharing spirit was at work in this man who refused to keep his bread to himself. The reader is amazed to find such a high moral and ethical standard extant in the ancient world, and presumably demonstrated by a man not of the Jewish race.

Again, the reason for Job's deliberate choice of this kind of ethical lifestyle is stated in terms of his assurance of God's reality. Job, who apparently had glimpsed something of God's glorious "splendor," could not and would not sin against that brightness.

> If I have put my trust in gold, or said to pure gold, "You are my security," if I have rejoiced over my great wealth, the fortune my hands have gained, if I have regarded the sun in its radiance or the moon moving in splendor, so that my heart was secretly enticed and my hand offered them a kiss of homage, then these also would be sins to be judged, for I would have been unfaithful to God on high. (Job 31:24–28)

Where does Job place his trust? Is it in his wealth? No, trust and security have never been lodged in material possessions, he insists. Job has not been greedy. The focus of his life has not been materialistic. Pride in possessions has not won him over and produced an arrogant miser. No, Job is not a worshipper of mammon. Nor is he an idolater. The sun may be radiant, the moon may have her splendor, but Job has never stooped to allow his admiration for these created bodies to become anything more than that. He has not worshipped the creature rather than the Creator. He is an ethical monotheist, who once again asserts that all of his actions are directed by his perspective of life lived before God, to whom Job is totally determined to remain faithful and loyal.

> If I have rejoiced at my enemy's misfortune or gloated over the trouble that came to him . . . (Job 31:29–30)

In Job's treatment of other people there was a noticeable New Testament element. He did not wish his enemies ill. Malignant malice seems to have been totally lacking in his character. Enemies he may have had, people who had decided they would not be his friends. But if trouble came to them, Job did not say, "Good! They got what was coming to them!" The inference is that he was sorry when his enemies suffered, wishing rather for their conversion into his friends.

> I have not allowed my mouth to sin by invoking a curse against his life . . . (Job 31:30)

It is not at all uncommon to hear men curse their enemies in our society. Curses are not reserved only for enemies, however. We have all heard people curse at other drivers, at bungled sports plays, at the weather, even at friends and family members. In fits of bad temper, some parents have been known to curse their own children. Mothers and fathers who do not pray at any other time call down heaven's wrath sometimes upon even their infant offspring, saying, "God damn you!" This is a terribly serious statement: it is a curse of the highest order. As believers we are glad God is not obliged to answer such requests. If God committed to perdition and damnation all who are so cursed by angry (and sometimes merely careless or joking) human beings—well, there are prayers God answers, and thankfully, there are prayers he ignores. The one who so prays is not ignored however, even though Heaven does not take the request seriously. "You shall not misuse the name of the Lord your God," said God (Exod 20:7), "Hallowed be your Name," said Jesus (Matt 6:9). Job indicates that he is well aware of the truth that to invoke a curse upon another—to wish another's harm and to call upon God to inflict such harm—is a sin.

Is there not a great need in our society to take God's name more seriously, to treat God and his character far more reverently? Do we not need to watch our language, knowing that our "speech betrays" us? In the marketplace there is plenty of cursing. This has been so throughout history. It was so in Job's day. Job, however, did not take part in it. Even his enemies were not the recipients of curses called down upon their heads. Job was a man of pure speech and possessed a spirit that was large-hearted and not revengeful.

> If the men of my household have never said, "who has not had his fill of Job's meat?"—but no stranger had to spend the night in the street, for my door was always open to the traveler. (Job 31:31–32)

Again the compassion of Job, the sharing liberality demonstrated often to those of his employ, and his hospitality manifested to travelers and strangers are expressed. "My door was always open to the traveler," he said. Job, you appeal to us more and more as a very human, approachable, thoughtful, kind-hearted, benevolent, and sensitive man. No wonder God was proud of you!

Before the Storms: Job Introduced and Praised   23

> If I have concealed my sin as men do, by hiding my guilt in my heart because I so feared the crowd and so dreaded the contempt of the clans that I kept silent and would not go outside . . . (Job 31:33–34)

Here is a reflection of Job's humble honesty. He indicates that he is not guiltless (he refers simply to "my sin . . . my guilt . . ."), but he has not sought to cover up his faults, or hide his shortcomings in a secret closet. Many people in high places in our land are frightened that the media might discover sins in their recent or not-so-recent past. Politicians and candidates for the highest offices in the land have been brought down by revelations unearthed by diligent reporters. Even well-known evangelists have tumbled from positions of respect and influence because of moral lapses that were hidden until uncovered by those who had reason to reveal their dark secrets.

Job confesses that he is a sinner. But he has not hidden his sin. He has openly sacrificed atonement offerings for his sin and guilt. He can truthfully say that he has nothing to hide. He has no fear that skeletons will be unearthed from his past that will be paraded before the world and used against him. What a testimony!

> Oh, that I had someone to hear me! I sign now my defense—let the Almighty answer me; let my accuser put his indictment in writing. Surely I would wear it on my shoulder, I would put it on like a crown. I would give him an account of my every step; like a prince I would approach him. (Job 31:35–37)

The anguish of Job overwhelms him; he breaks off his self-description with this ejaculatory plea for a listening ear, a fair trial, and an understanding judge. Job is not afraid to face even God, if it should be he who makes accusation against him. Job has summed up the case in his own favor, and is about ready to pronounce, "the defense rests!"

> If my land cries out against me and all its furrows are wet with tears, if I have devoured its yield without payment or broken the spirit of its tenants, then let briers come up instead of wheat and weeds instead of barley. The words of Job are ended. (Job 31:38–40)

Job's very last words. It is most fitting that they are the words of a lover of the soil, a man who is close to the earth, one who believes that the very ground can speak of the kindness or the cruelty of the man who has ploughed and planted her over and over again. Let the land speak for him, he pleads: she will defend him. If she does not, Job will accept her verdict, and will go down with her condemnation.

SUMMARY OF JOB'S CHARACTER

If we add up all of these qualities, qualities described by the author of the book, by the Lord himself, by Job's friends, and by his own testimony, we discover a man of genuine integrity. He is a godly man first of all, and a good man through and through.

Into the life of this good, godly man of integrity came a sudden and terrifying series of storms. It is extremely important to note at this point that the storm of suffering came upon Job, not because God was displeased with him, not because he needed correction, and not because he had sinned and needed divine chastisement. Surely if we take seriously the picture of the man we have seen presented to us thus far, we will agree that Job has done nothing amiss, nothing that would call down upon his head the wrath of the Almighty. On the contrary, Job is a man about whom only good can be said. If he must suffer, it is not because God has something against him. Why do bad things happen to good people? We will have to look for other reasons than chastisement, correction, or even motivational stimulus to character improvement in the case of Job.

Some authors cling to the idea that Job needed affliction to improve his character. Tabb has written a book whose subtitle quotes Job's brave words following the calamities he has experienced: "Should we accept only good things from the hand of God?" (Job 2:10). Tabb indicates by the use of these words that his thesis is that bad things come from God's hand, and his book tries to prove that bad things from God's hand are good things for God's servants, including Job. "Yet pain and suffering in the lives of Christ's followers can make it easier for us to crucify the flesh and follow Christ with single-minded devotion. Suffering also produces strength of character within us."[3] This may be true for some, but Job did not need bad things to improve his character.

---

3. Tabb, *Whirlwind*, 134. It seems to me that Tabb misses the point with his subtitle; he is quoting the [noble] words of a man who believes the bad things have come from the hand of God; but Job is ignorant of the malicious hand of Satan, the inflictor of bad things. Tabb misunderstands the reference to Christ in Heb 2:10: "In bringing many sons to glory, it was fitting that God . . . should make the author of their salvation perfect

STUDY QUESTIONS FOR CHAPTER 1

1. What impressions have you had with regard to the character of Job before entering upon this present study? Where did these impressions come from? Have any of them been challenged so far?

2. Do you agree that it is important to properly introduce Job before entering upon a discussion of suffering in the light of his experience? Why, or why not?

3. Make a list of Job's character traits. Is anything missing that would make him more human or understandable? In what ways is his character worthy of emulation? In what ways would you like to be like Job?

4. Some interpreters, as we have noted, are annoyed with Job's words about himself. They believe Job was demonstrating an arrogant spirit of self-righteousness, and perhaps this bragging spirit needed the corrective chastisement offered by his suffering. How would you respond to this line of thinking?

5. How can we account for a person of such noble character in such an ancient setting?

---

through suffering." The way to perfection, Tabb asserts, is through suffering. Therefore, he concludes, "why should we expect anything less in our own lives?" (p. 133). But I want to point out that Hebrews is speaking of Christ in his work as Savior; to be a perfect and complete Savior he had to suffer. Suffering and saviorhood are inseparable. But suffering and perfection of character are not at issue in this Hebrews passage. If suffering were necessary for character perfection, the holiest people of all would be those in perdition! And Job before the attacks would not be called blameless. Christians are called upon to suffer for their faith, and faith, tried by fire, can triumph. Of this fact the pre-Christian Job is a sterling example. Tabb's book is about the necessity of pain and suffering for Christian character development. He says, "Pain and suffering pry my hands off everything in which I trust so that I might trust in Christ alone" (p. 154). True as this insight sometimes is, it is not what the book of Job is about.

2

The Storms Break: God's Servant Tried and Trusted

GOD'S SERVANT TRIED

OUT OF NOWHERE CAME calamity. Everything was going well, and suddenly everything went wrong. In rapid succession the loss of farms, fields, buildings, livestock, and servants, everything Job could call his own, gone. All (his wife seems to have survived) gone. And his children were gone, too, those for whom he had prayed, perhaps that very morning, for God's protection to rest upon them. And without warning they were all taken in a freak accident. Adding injury to insult, Job's health suddenly and mysteriously failed—he was stricken with pain and agony—apparently a skin disease erupted all over his body, causing a loss of appetite, a loss of weight, and a loss of physical attractiveness to such a degree that when his friends came to visit him and comfort him, they were unable to recognize him, so great was his disfigurement.[1]

In what state of mind can we expect to find Job after this entire barrage of agony? How will he ever manage to hold sanity together after experiencing loss upon loss of such magnitude? And what about his faith now? Can his piety survive all these blows? Will all of this agony and pain and sorrow and anguish crush him to the degree that he will give up on God and decide that since he has lost everything else he might as well give up on God, on goodness, on life itself? His wife seems to think

---

1. Strahan, *Book of Job*, 45–46, identifies Job's physical malady as a form of leprosy, "called elephantiasis, the symptoms of which correspond with the numerous indications scattered through the book: Itching (2:8), sores breaking and hardening again (7:5), the blackening and eating away of the skin and the members (30:30 and 18:30), shocking changes in appearance (2:12), violent pains (2:13, 16:6), gnawing in the limbs (30:17), . . . emaciation (19:20), fever (30:27, 30), sleeplessness and terrifying dreams (7:4, 14), weeping eyes and dim sight (16:16), bad breath (19:17)."

he need not be expected to take any more punishment. "Give up your faith, curse God, deny God, and die," she advises, perhaps suggesting that suicide would seem to be a wise option for her miserable husband.[2]

We are not left in doubt as to Job's character. The book provides abundant information about that. Neither are we left to wonder how he would respond to all the slings and arrows of outrageous fortune that were thrust upon him.

The major portion of the book is taken up with Job's words, words addressed to his friends, words uttered to himself, and words aimed at the ear of the Lord. They are speeches full of the questions of a very perplexed man. "Why is all this happening; why to me, and why now? What happened to the good old days, when things were going so well, and God's blessing was so evidently upon my life? What in all the world did I do to deserve all the pain that I have been called upon to endure?" These and ever so many more questions plague Job. His friends have no satisfactory answers for him. And for a good portion of the story the Lord remains silent to him. So Job must question, must suffer, must wait—and must endure.

And endure he does. For all of his questioning, he does not lapse into unbelief. Never once does he doubt the existence of God. Never once does he suggest that although it seems that he is gaining very little for his life of goodness, kindness, and integrity, he should abandon his determination to live righteously no matter what comes his way. Job has lost everything that can be taken away from a man. Everything. But he does not let go of that which no one can take from him without his permission. His character as a servant of God remains, and, he says, will remain though death finally overtakes him.

THE SOURCE OF THE STORMS

Where did the storms come from? Why did they come? Was there any reason for all of these misfortunes and disasters? Again, there are some answers suggested in the first two chapters. They are answers known to

---

2. Strahan, *Book of Job*, 46, writes, "The distracted woman, seeing her husband suffer so terribly and so hopelessly, suggests that an instantaneous death, such as might follow blasphemy, would be better than a lingering, painful, loathsome end. Some readers hold that Job thinks of suicide, suggested to him by his wife; but, while that way of deliverance would have seemed natural to a Roman, there is no evidence that it ever presented itself to Job, one who recognized that God alone had the power and right of life and death."

us as the readers of the book, but we must remember that they are answers apparently unavailable to Job, right down to the end of the story.

> One day the angels came to present themselves before the Lord, and Satan also came with them. The Lord said to Satan, "Where have you come from?"
>
> Satan answered the Lord, "From roaming through the earth and going back and forth in it." Then the Lord said to Satan, "Have you considered my servant Job? There is no one on earth like him; he is blameless and upright, a man who fears God and shuns evil."
>
> "Does Job fear God for nothing?" Satan replied. "Have you not put a hedge around him and his household and everything he has? You have blessed the work of his hands, so that his flocks and herds are spread throughout the land. But stretch out your hand and strike everything he has, and he will surely curse you to your face."
>
> The Lord said to Satan, "Very well, then, everything he has is in your hands, but on the man himself do not lay a finger."
>
> Then Satan went out from the presence of the Lord ...
>
> On another day the angels came to present themselves before the Lord, and Satan came with them to present himself before him. And the Lord said to Satan, "Where have you come from?"
>
> Satan answered the Lord, "From roaming through the earth and going back and forth in it."
>
> Then the Lord said to Satan, "Have you considered my servant Job? There is no one on earth like him; he is blameless and upright, a man who fears God and shuns evil. And he still maintains his integrity, though you incited me against him to ruin him without any reason."
>
> "Skin for skin!" Satan replied. "A man will give all he has for his own life. But stretch out your hand and strike his flesh and bones, and he will surely curse you to your face."
>
> The Lord said to Satan, "Very well, then, he is in your hands; but you must spare his life."
>
> So Satan went out from the presence of the Lord and afflicted Job with painful sores from the soles of his feet to the top of his head ... (Job 1:6–12 and 2:1–7)

Give Satan His Due!

Satan, of course, is behind all the dreadful events that transpired in Job's experience. His presence in the council of heaven is a mystery. His conversations with the Lord are a problem to us. But that is not because we do not understand what these two beings, the One who is the author of all that is good and perfect, the other the initiator of all that is evil and hellish, have to say to each other.[3]

    3. It is difficult to understand or agree with the position taken by Ellison regarding the part played by Satan in the troubles of Job: "It is not unfair to say that the vast majority of Christians either fly in the face of revelation and experience and deny the existence of Satan, or attribute to him such wide-reaching power and authority as to become virtual dualists in their religion. The teaching of scripture is clear that nothing exists without God's will and permission. All power and authority are derived from Him. Whatever the position, and power of Satan, he is God's creation, his power is derived from God, and willingly or unwillingly he is working out God's purposes. This is clearly seen in his conversation with God about Job. It is usual to explain Job's sufferings by the malignity of Satan, but this is obviously false. Satan cannot even mention Job, for he has no accusation against him, until God invites him to do so. Equally, he has no power over Job or his possessions until God gives it him. So it is clear that, while God uses Satan's malignity, the origins of Job's sufferings goes back to God himself, and no explanation of God's action is ever offered" (Ellison, *From Tragedy to Triumph*, 25). It seems to me that attributing misfortune to God's inscrutable sovereignty is precisely Job's greatest problem. Many writers play down Satan's role in bringing about Job's agonies. Satan is merely God's tool they say, "God's servant," but really the calamities come, if only indirectly, from the Omnipotent One. Even so fine a commentary as that of Francis Andersen fails here: "The contribution of the Satan to the action of the book is minor. His place in its theology is even less. In the subsequent discussions the misfortunes of men are never traced to a diabolical foe, and it is impossible to believe that the purpose of this tremendous book is to teach us an explanation of evil that Job and his friends never think of, namely that human suffering is caused by the Devil. The Satan does not appear again after Job 2:7" (Andersen, *Job*, 83). But consider Fyall, *My Eyes Have Seen You*, 20, who writes, "Satan is not simply a minor figure who has a walk-on part in chapters one and two and then disappears from the action. Rather the battle with evil is a major motif of the book as a whole." Fyall, citing numerous biblical and Ancient Near Eastern texts, identifies "Behemoth [as] a figure of death, and ... Leviathan [as] a guise of Satan" (p. 18). Of course I recognize that there is a development in the unfolding revelation about Satan from the Old through the New Testament, but that is not because Satan has changed; it is not a lesser Satan who plagues Job, as some assert. E.g. Gibson, *Job*, 12, says, "What are we to make of this sinister and busy figure? The Satan is a nasty piece of work, brazen and impertinent toward God, and cynical and sneering about men. These are traits he carries with him in his subsequent career as God's enemy or opposite, when as Satan ... he will have his own "kingdom" as opposed to God's ... But here he is patently not yet God's enemy in that full sense, but still very much his subordinate ... So there is only one possible conclusion: Satan is, in this story ... still an extension of God. He represents an aspect of God's providence: that side of him which, for whatever reason, visits suffering upon human beings; that side of him which is responsible for

God holds up his servant before the devil as a model of righteousness and godly piety. Apparently Job is a paragon of all that Satan detests. Satan refuses to believe that a human being can be anything but like himself—hypocritical and dishonestly deceitful. Humanity is basically evil, he believes, and all humans are essentially corruptible.

Satan seems convinced that not even God's servants are immune to self-serving. Job is a good man because he is a blessed man. Take away the blessing, Satan urges, and the goodness will depart with it. Faith will go with them, and God's servant will be no more and no less than another defeated, discouraged, despairing, hopeless human being. Beat a person down with trouble and sorrow, and you will drive the faith and hope completely out of him or her. No person, not even the best, can stand up to a relentless barrage of satanic buffeting. Such is Satan's philosophy of human nature! Such is his opinion of the quality of faith possessed by God's servant

Is this true? Was Satan correct in his assessment of human character? Is it true that all people, even godly people, even the godliest of people, have their price? Pay them enough and they will be good. Take away enough and they will break and fall. Can faith stand the test of circumstances that are all but unbearable? Do piety and purity, godliness and goodness, depend for their existence upon pleasantness of living

---

the evil and tragedy which afflict the lives of men." Is this attribution of evil to God not Job's major dilemma? Why do writers like Gibson continue to insist on minimizing Satan's objective, personal existence, while convicting God of direct responsibility for Job's calamities? It seems to me that Gibson inadvertently identifies modern thinkers with the very problem we are trying to correct as we take the Prologue and Satan's active part in Job's troubles seriously and literally. Gibson says, "we still find it exceedingly difficult to sanction the Old Testament's robust habit of attributing evil to God's direct will. We prefer to avoid the issue by having the devil, or some impersonal force, perform the evil, and God simply permit it. But that is in theory only. What do we do in practice? When trouble comes our way we do not usually wonder what the Devil, or the principalities and powers have to do with it, but in pain and perplexity we ask what God is up to. As in so many other spheres, our practice is perhaps more revealing than our theory. It shows we are not so far removed from Job's world as we might suppose" (p. 14). Many point out that the designation for the enemy in Job is "the Satan," and suggest that he is not the same as the Devil. Mason, *Gospel according to Job*, 28, assists us here: "Just as the term 'Christ' (or 'anointed one') does not come to assume personal weight until the advent of Jesus, so only in the New Testament does the shadowy figure of 'the satan' step fully out of the wings. This personalization of evil began to take shape during the intertestamental period, but the revelation remained blurred until Jesus met Satan face-to-face in the wilderness, and then proceeded to expose the Devil's dark identity and all his evil works before the world."

and smooth sailing over untroubled seas? Or do faith, hope and love abide, disasters notwithstanding? *Can* they abide?

These are important questions. They are tremendously meaningful considerations. What will the man or woman of faith do when trouble comes, and comes to stay for an agonizingly long time? Is trouble necessarily a sign that faith has already departed or is at least in a state of severe disrepair? Is faith always rewarded materially in the here and now? Are God's servants exempt from trouble? From big trouble? From tragedy? And if not, how do believers react and respond when things go very wrong? Do God's servants react to tragedy differently than those who are unbelievers? Does it even matter if one is a believer if troubles come to everybody? Can faith be put to the test in the furnace of affliction, and will it survive, and even be strengthened in the process? What a host of questions arise as one ponders the story of the breaking of the storm upon Job!

Why do good people suffer? How do good people suffer? Can good people suffer grievously without ceasing to be good, and godly? These are some of the most important questions thoughtful people can ever ask. And many insights are offered to the careful student of the book of Job that aid in the formulation of answers.

Indeed, we might not have known the answer to some of these questions if this book were not in the Bible. Had God not allowed Satan to barrage Job with his series of incredible assaults, and had not the story of Job's victorious endurance been preserved for us, we might well wonder whether faith can be severely subjected to the limit of human endurance and not be destroyed in the process. The test was applied by Satan, but trust was placed by God in his servant. Did God trust his servant in vain?

GOD'S SERVANT TRUSTED

God trusted his servant. That seems like a strange thing to say about any biblical account.[4] The Bible is a book that directs people to trust in

---

4. Strahan, *Book of Job*, 37, writes, "While the Satan is a skeptic . . . God, who is Job's Maker, is, on the other hand, a believer. He stands by Job, puts a stake on him and authorizes Satan to try him. It is obvious that the question of Job's disinterestedness, once raised, can be settled only by the way of experiment, and Jahweh, listening to his subordinate's objection, is obliged, against his inclination, to consent to the trial. It is arbitrary to assume that there is any thought of deepening Job's piety or purifying his character by suffering. This is to confuse the issue. The experiment takes place, not

God. We do not expect to find a book contained in the Scriptures that describes God as placing his trust in a human being! But Job is just such a story. God is sure of his servant. He believes that Job will be true to what he believes about God and righteousness no matter what happens to him.

As noted earlier, it is surprising to find God praising his servant. It is strange to overhear God as he brags about a mere mortal to the council of heaven. It is even more unusual, almost unbelievable, to catch a glimpse behind the scenes as God dares to place his trust in the integrity of his servant.

Satan has made a serious charge—no human will serve God voluntarily and freely. All people are innately and incurably selfish. Take away the hedge of divine protection and largesse, and God's servant will tumble from the wall of belief like Humpty Dumpty—and no one will be able to put the pieces back together again![5]

The Almighty takes these charges seriously. The only way to prove them false is to allow Job to be tested. Will faith collapse if the divine protection is removed? The only way to be sure is to remove it. Allow the adversary to do his worst to Job. Prove to him that this good and goodly man will persevere to the end. Let Job be tested; God is sure of the outcome. God is sure Job will pass the exam. He trusts his servant. Such trust on the part of God himself seems in retrospect to have been

---

for the sufferer's moral good, but in order to silence doubt as to the sincerity of his goodness."

5. Wood, *Job and the Human Situation*, 37, speaks of Satan about to inflict physical suffering upon Job and being ordered by God not to take Job's life: "[Satan] attempts to inveigle God into doing his dirty work! He suggests that God should strike Job . . . The interesting thing to notice is that God does not even consider this cunning suggestion for one moment. Once more the defect of cynicism is revealed; it is no more able to understand God's ways with man than it is to appreciate human integrity. Quite curtly and with clearly defined limits, Satan is given permission to deal with Job as he thinks fit for the purposes of the second trial. Obviously, if the trial is to be a trial and not a sordid murder, Job must be kept alive. With that one proviso, Satan hurries off with indecent haste to afflict Job." One author who indicates the tendency to de-emphasize the activity of Satan in Job, and thus in the human experience of suffering, is Kent, *Job our Contemporary*. This is a very helpful volume in many respects, but contains no mention whatever of the Satanic influences abroad in the world. Kent mentions the name of Satan only once in the book, (p. 40), and the reference is simply to God's words of praise regarding Job uttered to him.

an unspeakable compliment paid to a mere mortal.[6] Consider the following personal illustration of trust in the midst of testing.

An Illustration of Trust

As part of the requirements for graduation with a Master's Degree from Wilfrid Laurier University, I had to take an oral comprehensive examination on all the History courses I had completed at the graduate level. This is standard procedure in graduate schools, and I have been through the process several times since at different levels. It is a somewhat unpleasant but necessary rite of passage in scholastic circles.

My graduate advisor was an old professor named Joseph Braun. Dr. Braun knew more about the Middle Ages in Europe than anyone I have ever met. He was a dear man and a demanding professor. He greatly encouraged me to take the exam and to go from there into doctoral studies, which I eventually did. Dr. Braun has been dead for several years now. So much wisdom died with him!

An hour or so before the examination, I went to Dr. Braun's office and he and I talked about history for some time. Then my old professor, who knew I was a Christian, said, "Tom, do you want to pray?" We hadn't talked very much about spiritual things up to that point, but I eagerly accepted his invitation, and we prayed about that exam.

In the exam room, I found that I was on the "hot seat," surrounded by the professors under whom I had studied. They were joined by the head of the Psychology Department, who was to be the chairperson, and by an outside examiner from a neighboring university. Several others were present as observers. Dr. Braun was seated among the questioners, but he had been placed as far from me as possible. I could hardly see him, much less communicate with him. To say the least, I was terrified. Many graduate students reading this account will completely identify with this experience.

The exam began, and I must say it seemed to be going very well. Each faculty member in turn questioned me on my knowledge of the past. Then the outside examiner spoke up and posed some particularly difficult problems for me to solve. I glanced at Dr. Braun. He was looking

---

6. Waltke, *Old Testament Theology*, 932, says it well: "God's challenge to Satan to prove God's faith in him despite counterevidence shows that *I AM* uses mortals to validate truths about himself . . . History is the crucible of truth, conferring awful dignity upon mortals."

sympathetically at me, but of course was unable to speak to me. I was on my own. He knew it and so did I. I wanted to say, "Dr. Braun, come to my rescue!" But I could not. He, undoubtedly, wanted to interject, "Please, let me answer that question for Mr. Dow." But he could not. Dr. Braun had to trust me. For this test to be genuine and legitimate, he had to remain silent. To speak up for my encouragement or in my defense would have been to render the examination forfeit. As agonizing as it must have been for him, Dr. Braun said nothing; he simply trusted me to defend his integrity as a professor, and mine as a budding scholar. He trusted me because he believed I would not fail. He had done his part in the classroom. I had learned so much from him. Now this teaching-learning process was being put to the test. Would I come through the exam intact?

Apparently Joseph Braun thought so. When I think about it now, I realize it was he who urged me to take the test, and even arranged for it to be held. For some reason he believed in me. He allowed me to be examined, somewhat painfully, because he dared to believe I could take it. I had the knowledge; I could articulate it under pressure. I did pass the exam. And back in his office after it was all over, Joe Braun clasped my hand and said, sincerely, "I knew you would do it!"

The Evil Examiner

This personal illustration is given with the realization that it falls far short in comparison to the intensity, gravity, and far-reaching significance of Job's ordeal. That said, it was in like manner, but with far more serious implications, that God allowed his servant to be tested. Satan, the archenemy of God and of all true believers, conducted the examination, and it was a fearsome test. Satan is real. He does exist. He is the accuser of God's people, the source of all lies and deceit, the author of all evil, the one who holds the power of death and dispenses it. How wicked he is! How he desires to sift us like wheat—to have us, and hold us, and destroy us.

Hear God ask Satan, "Where have you been?" in Job 2:2. We know where Satan has been and what he has been doing. He has been wreaking havoc upon the family and possessions of Job. Yet listen to his answer, filled with all innocence and deceit: "Walking to and fro in the earth and going up and down in it." "Where have you been, Satan?" We know where he was. God knew as well. God knows and we know that all disasters, calamities, devastations, all manner of evil, and tragic occurrences are the work of him who is the Prince of the Power of the Air. Where was Satan? As a roaring lion he was going about seeking and devouring. And he still exists and is still intent on his fiendish work of destroying God's work and workmanship.

The Bible tells us that Christ came into the world to "destroy the devil's works" (1 John 3:8). What are the devil's "works?" In 1 John 3:8 we read, "He who does what is sinful is of the devil, because the devil has been sinning from the beginning." Sin is the work of the devil; wherever there is evil and iniquity, the devil is at work, for sin is his work, and he is the author of it. In John 8:44, we are told that the devil "was a murderer from the beginning, not holding to the truth, for there is no truth in him. When he lies, he speaks his native language, for he is a liar and the father of lies." Here we learn that death is one of the devil's works; he is the destroyer of life (cf. Heb 2:14, "so that by his [Christ's] death he might destroy him who holds the power of death—that is, the devil"). He is the father of lies, the destroyer of the truth. He lied to Adam and Eve about God in the Garden of Eden, ("Did God really say . . . ?), and he lied to God about Job, ("he will surely curse you to your face"). Satan put it into the heart of Judas to betray Jesus: he is the author of all betrayal, seeking to destroy love. The devil's work is to destroy life, truth, and love in the world. Jesus has brought life out of death, truth out of falsehood, light out of darkness, love out of betrayal. He is the way, the truth and the life; he destroys the works of the devil as he shares life and truth and love with his own. Because of Christ's power we are able to resist the devil, and we know that when we do he will flee from us. It is nevertheless still the case that Satan has power to afflict the believer (as well as the unbeliever), to torment and oppress us, and to use his arsenal against us to attempt our downfall as he attempted Job's.

The apostle Paul calls Satan our adversary, and reminds us to be vigilant, on guard, well armed (Eph 6:10–18), knowing the devil's schemes (2 Cor 2:11). Troubles that come our way may come directly from Satan's hand, with the sole purpose, not of refining us, but of destroying us. If we learn anything from Job, it is not to ascribe these things to God as though they came from his good hand, but to recognize their source, and with God's grace to conquer the enemy by overcoming the circumstances, overcoming by the "blood of the Lamb and the word of our testimony" (see Rev 12:11).

God trusted Job, and his trust was not misplaced. Does God still place his trust in his servants? Does he count on us to bear all things, for his glory? Can we be trusted? Can God entrust his reputation to us? Can we be trusted to endure and maintain our integrity and faith when tried, when tested, and even when called upon to undergo severe suffering?

The depiction in the book of Job of Satan's attitude toward humanity, God, and God's servant, and the description of his power in inflicting evil upon human beings, needs to be taken far more seriously than it often is. It is not myth. It is reality. The devil seeks nothing less than the destruction of God's servants. He is out to ensure that all who take his examination fail it miserably. Some have. God was sure that Job would not.

Can trouble bring down God's servant? Is the fall of the faithful inevitable given enough satanic oppression and pressure? Satan said, "Yes! And I can prove it." God said, "No! Here is my servant. I will take away for a time my hedge of protection. I will stand in the shadows for a while and be silent. Test Job. Examine him. For the sake of all the watching world of humans and angels,[7] let him be subjected to the worst you can conjure from your bag of diabolical tricks. He will stand. I believe in him. I trust Job. His faith can conquer. My servant will come through it all, triumphantly!" At the end of the story of Job, after the enemy has done his worst and Job has insisted on maintaining his integrity, we find God still pleased with his servant. Four times in the last chapter of the book God refers to Job as "my servant." Do I hear the echo of Dr. Braun's congratulatory, "I knew you would do it"?

So the storms broke; the examination was conducted in all deadly seriousness. Job was altogether unaware of the incredible importance of what was transpiring. Had he had some notion of Satan's plans and God's permittings, the devil might have cried, hypocritically, "Foul!" Job must not know of the test, lest he determine to be faithful, knowing the limits God has placed upon the enemy. For his integrity to triumph, Job must endure the silence of his God and the agonizing surprises of his

---

7. It is surely for our sakes, and for the sake of the heavenly onlookers, (cf. Eph 3:10–11, "His [God's] intent was that now, through the church, the manifold wisdom of God should be made known to the rulers and authorities in the heavenly realms, according to his eternal purpose . . ." We really have very little comprehension of the cosmic significance of our struggles as believers!), and not for Satan's sake—God owes him no arguments or apologetic proofs.

tormenter; and endure he did, but not without baring his soul in anguish as he cried out for meaning and understanding.

The agonies of a person under severest stress are revealed in the speeches of Job during the storms, and to his reactions and those of his "friends" throughout the ordeal we now turn our attention.

REACTIONS TO THE STORMS

On the one hand, Job's reactions are very human. Job is a mortal and he responds like one. Beyond this, however, Job reacts as a human being who is also a believer. There is an added dimension to Job's being, something that sets him apart from reacting only in a human way. This added dimension, of course, is the fact that he is a committed servant of God. He possesses faith as well as feeling. He is able to rationalize as well as any intelligent person, but in addition he is able to call upon the resources of his understanding and experience of the unseen world. The following chapter will describe Job's human (nonetheless God-conscious) reactions as they are revealed in his speeches, and will seek to interact with the ideas presented in these reactions. The analysis of the speeches would not be complete, however, without considering the reactions of Job, the man of faith. It is our contention that it is Job's faith that brings him to victory. As the New Testament proclaims, "This is the victory that has overcome the world, even our faith" (1 John 5:4).

STUDY QUESTIONS FOR CHAPTER 2

1. Ponder carefully each question posed in the second paragraph of this chapter. What are your initial answers to these questions? How important are these issues?

2. What do you think about the section above entitled, "God's Servant Trusted"? Does God trust his servants? You and me? How can we be worthy of this honor?

3. Is it fair to give the devil so much credit for Job's troubles? Think about and discuss in more detail than is offered here the Bible's teaching about Satan.

3

During the Storms:
Reactions of Job—A Person Like Us

How did Job respond to all the calamity through which he was passing? From the first two chapters of *Job* we know that he nobly accepted without question the circumstances that came his way. "Naked I came from my mother's womb, and naked I will depart. The Lord gave and the Lord has taken away; may the name of the Lord be praised" (Job 1:21). Brave words indeed! "Shall we accept good from God and not trouble?" (Job 2:10) he asked his skeptical wife. These are words full of faith and of resignation to what he perceived to be a divine visitation of woe upon him.

WHAT JOB DOES NOT KNOW

Remember, however, that Job is not aware of the source of his misery. He attributes all that happens to him to the direct activity of God. There seems to be no notion of a satanic source of evil and torment in his theology. Job and his friends believe in the absolute sovereignty of God; all that happens in life, whether good or bad, comes from God's hand. This ideology forms a large part of Job's dilemma. He believes in God, and never ceases to believe. He believes in God's greatness and power and almighty overlordship of events. Surely he possesses a satisfactory view of God, his attributes and his omnipotence. What Job does not possess, however, is an adequate explanation for the existence and pervasiveness of evil in the world, and of the fact that evil can be attributed to someone other than God when it invades human experience. We know who is to blame for so much of the iniquity and disjointedness of the world around us. We know that Satan, though his time is short, still exerts great evil influence all over the world. We know, however, that his doom is sure, and that on the side of the Master, we are safe from his devices. We will live to see his ultimate downfall.[1]

In the dialogues that form the middle part of the book and divide the Prologue and the Epilogue, Job's brave words sometimes become questioning words. Reflecting on his continual suffering, he probes the implications of his theological assumptions, and he finds the analysis very disturbing. In his agony and desperation, Job questions God's dealings with him in ways that come close (but never cross the line) to blasphemy.

> Surely, O God, you have worn me out; you have devastated my entire household. You have bound me—and it has become a witness; my gauntness rises up and testifies against me. God assails me and tears me in his anger and gnashes his teeth at me; my opponent fastens on me his piercing eyes ... God has turned me over to evil men and thrown me into the clutches of the wicked. All was well with me, but he shattered me; he seized me by the neck and crushed me. He has made me his target; his archers surround me. Without pity he pierces my kidneys and spills my gall on the ground. Again and again he bursts upon me; he rushes at me like a warrior. (Job 16:7–14)

God is punishing him mercilessly, he cries. God is using him for target practice. God is shooting the arrows that are destroying him. God has made him, prospered him, and brought him to a position of prominence, for the sole purpose of bringing him down and destroying him. It is the Lord who will not give him a moment's peace, no, not so much as time to breathe. God watches over him every moment to see how he may add to the torment:

> Does it please you to oppress me, to spurn the work of your hands, while you smile on the schemes of the wicked? ... Your hands shaped me and made me. Will you now turn and destroy me? Remember that you molded me like clay. Will you now turn me to dust again? ... You gave me life and showed me kindness, and in your providence watched over my spirit. But this is what you concealed in your heart ..." (Job 10:3–9, 12–13)

---

1. Strahan, *Book of Job*, 100, says, "The very strictness of Job's monotheism is what makes the problem of evil so baffling and tormenting to him. He has no Gnostic Demiurge, no Christian devil, no scientific second causes, no scheme of providence to help him to solve the riddle of the universe."

And in the midst of all this, Job indicates his inability to understand this (as he sees it) dark side of Deity, "If it is not he, then who is it?"(Job 9:24).

OUR DIALOGUE WITH JOB

As readers of the book of Job, we would like to answer Job's question. We would give anything to be able to become part of the story so that we could inform Job concerning that of which he is unaware. "Job," we would say, "stop blaming the Lord for all of this. There is another power at work in the world. There is a Satan. There is an Evil One, and he it is who is directly responsible for your woes. You are blaming the wrong party. You are not giving Satan credit due to him." Such dialogue is most unfair to Job, we realize. He lived when he did and followed all the light he had. These dialogues with Job are really with ourselves. We have more light than Job had and when storms come to us we have brighter resources at our disposal to draw upon when we ask the questions he did and respond as humans in similar ways to Job. But let us continue our conversation with this very vulnerable sufferer.

"You are continually asking, where is God, Why does he not speak to me, speak for me, defend me and vindicate me? Job, he *has* spoken for you! He has spoken about you! He has praised you in heaven. He has bragged about you to the angels. And even now his eye is upon you. It is not the eye of the tormentor; it is the eye of one who trusts and believes in you. If he is silent, it is only the silence of his confidence in you. Believe us, Job, God is for you!

"Certainly your circumstances seem to say otherwise, but things are not always as they seem to be. All of life is out of order, because Satan is the master of disorder. But God is there with you. He is silent, but if you will endure to the end, he will speak!

"Why is this happening to you? What are all of these troubles meant to accomplish? The answer, Job, is that they are intended to break you down, and destroy your faith, your hope, and your determination to be God's good servant. There is no corrective purpose in them. The Lord is not chastening you. The Lord is not testing you; he trusts you. God trusts you to show to the believers of the ages that faith can triumph over circumstances.

"The Lord *is* satisfied with you. He believes you can be subjected to the worst that can come to humans, and that you will endure it all with faith and hope. God has allowed you to be tried and afflicted; part of the agony is his own invisible silence. But you will see him! You will hear his voice! We know, for we have read your story from beginning to end. And he knows the end from the beginning far better than we ever will. Trust on, Job. Hang on, and don't give in to the temptation to say, 'That's it. I can't bear any more. There is No One there. There is only pain, misery, and a useless life.' Job, don't give up on God and goodness. Seek first his kingdom, his righteousness..."

We know how the story ends, don't we? We know that Job did endure. He questioned, he agonized, he cried out to God for answers and for meaning. The answers were not forthcoming, but he endured anyway. His words in chapter 27 are words of determination; the nobility and the bravery have triumphed. Essentially he is saying, "Even though I die I will not give up my integrity. To the end I will cling to what I know to be the truth (cf. Job 27:5). The best thing to do, no matter what, is to retain the confidence I have always had—'The fear of the Lord, that is wisdom, and to shun evil is understanding!'" (Job 28:28).

These noble words were his last words, but in the course of his dialogues with his three friends he offered other sentiments that were not so noble. Other reactions surfaced, and they are the reactions typical of all human beings who are suffering and experiencing incredible pain and loss.

JOB'S HUMAN REACTIONS TO THE STORM OF TROUBLES

A study of the poetical portions of the book reveals at least thirty reactions to suffering coming from the lips of Job. Some of them were positive, as we have noted, and some were negatively conditioned by Job's ignorance of the details of the drama in which he was unwittingly the chief actor, and by his sheer agony of body and mind. Just as we interjected our ideas and attitudes into the story in the previous section, so it will be our opportunity to dialogue with Job as he reveals his feelings to us in his speeches. We will begin with a study of his reactions as a person who is very human. These reactions have little of faith or hope about them. Our examination will continue, however, with a study of his responses as a human being who is primarily a person of faith. These reactions—and they are surprisingly numerous as we shall see—are filled with courage and hope. Armed with these latter convictions, Job is able to triumph.

Job's "faith reactions" will be treated in detail in the next chapter. The following paragraphs discuss his reactions as a mere mortal.

Reaction #1: "I wish I'd never been born."

> May the day of my birth perish, and the night it was said, "A boy is born!" That day—may it turn to darkness; may God above not care about it; may no light shine upon it. May darkness and deep shadow claim it once more; may a cloud settle over it; may blackness overwhelm its light. That night—may thick darkness seize it; may it not be included among the days of the year nor be entered in any of the months. (Job 3:3–6)

In this his first monologue in the poetical section of the book, Job curses the day of his birth. He does not curse God; he does not sink into unbelief or disobedience. He just longs for death and an end to excruciating physical and emotional pain. Poetically, this wish for an end to suffering is expressed as a tirade against his birthday. The desire is unrealistic, unachievable, mere wishful thinking. It does illustrate the seriousness of his situation, the desperate anguish of his thought processes, and the intense humanity of this lonely sufferer.

Several verses in the latter part of the chapter reveal something of Job's concept of death and the afterlife. In the grave the wicked "cease from turmoil, and there the weary are at rest. Captives also enjoy their ease; they no longer hear the slave driver's shout. The small and great are there, and the slave is freed from his master" (Job 3:17–19). For this rest from toil Job longs. Who can blame him? When we hear this kind of reasoning from the lips of sufferers in our generation, let us not be surprised or overly judgmental. As with Job, the words may be pathetic and sorrowful. But they are not deserving of our censure, nor do they indicate a lack of God-pleasing faith.

Suffering believers may assure us that they rue the day of their birth. They may tell us that they long for death. We may be tempted to argue with them, to warn them that these thoughts are unacceptable theologically. Believers ought not to question their existence, for to do so is to question the One who brought them into existence. But we must learn to hold our tongues and theologize when it is appropriate. When a suffering human being is pouring out anguish in unreasonable, perhaps irrational sentiments, let us, like Job's friends on their best behavior, remain mercifully silent.

Reaction #2: "I knew something like this would happen!"

> What I feared has come upon me; what I dreaded has happened to me. (Job 3:25)

How often have we heard this sentiment coming from the lips of someone passing through a period of misfortune? The idea seems to be that everything was going well, too well. Good times, smooth sailing, these are the exception. Life is basically hard, and a spell of good times must always be followed by a period of troubles.

Job, we would like to caution you at this point. Really, the caution is directed at ourselves. Must we see life as basically tragic? Must we so expect misfortune that when it does visit us we intimate that we thought it would come sooner? There is a slight trace of superstition here, which asserts that when things are going well, we ought to beware; the fates are granting us a calm before the storm that will inevitably come crashing down on our heads. May we be delivered from this kind of thinking. Job can be forgiven for saying many things that would be unacceptable coming from those who will learn from his experience. The next time I am tempted to say, "I knew this would happen," may I remember Job, and be still.

Job's friend Eliphaz is even more pessimistic about humanity and about life when he utters words that are very negative and basically untrue, but that nevertheless find themselves enshrined in many contemporary funeral meditations: "For hardship does not spring from the soil, nor does trouble sprout from the ground, Yet man is born to trouble as surely as sparks fly upward" (Job 5:6–7). These words epitomizing the inevitability of human misery and woe were not particularly helpful to Job, nor are they to suffering people today!

Reaction #3: "I can't handle this!"

> What strength do I have that I should still hope? What prospects, that I should be patient? Do I have the strength of stone? Is my flesh bronze? Do I have any power to help myself, now that success has been driven from me? (Job 6:11–13)

Job wonders if he has the strength to make it. And many facing a serious operation or some other testing situation echo his words and thoughts: "I don't think I can handle this. I just couldn't handle that." Despite his fears, Job could handle it. He did handle it, he did make it. Examine your conversations. Do you find yourself facing hard things and turning away? I just can't! I can't go to that hospital to visit my friend with cancer. I can't go to that funeral home. I can't talk to that grieving person. I can't face this grueling move, or change, or operation, or family crisis. I can't.

Yes you can. With God you can. And with God you will. Remember what Paul said. "I can do all things . . ." That sounds quite egotistical and arrogant. But Paul did not stop there. "I can do all things," he said, "through Christ who strengthens me!" (Phil 4:13). That's not egoism or arrogance. That is confident faith in the power of Christ to help me cope with all things, and to handle whatever comes. Believers passing through great sorrows and stresses may echo Job's words, "I just can't handle this." It may be that medical help is needed, or psychological counseling, or sleep, or time away from the stressful situation, but what is most needed is confidence in God to help with the handling.

Incidentally, there is a verse in this sixth chapter of Job that contains some food for thought on the theme of friendship. In Job 6:14, Job says, "A despairing man should have the devotion of his friends, even though he forsakes the fear of the Almighty." Job knows his words are like wind, raw and raging. He knows that his thoughts, the thoughts of a man gone mad with pain, are wild thoughts. He really does not need reasoned arguments in the midst of his despair. He only wants, and desperately needs, real friends who will stay with him, and sympathize with him till the wildness subsides.

Unfortunately, the ideas of his three visitors on the subject of friendship are rather different than those expressed by Job in this verse. What kind of friend am I to one passing through a valley of shadows? What kind of friend are you?

Reaction #4: "What did I do to deserve this?"

> Is there any wickedness on my lips? Can my mouth not discern malice? (Job 6:30). I loathe my very life; therefore I will give free rein to my complaint and speak out in the bitterness of my soul. I will say to God: Do not condemn me, but tell me what charges you have against me. (Job 10:1–2)

Job wonders, and wonders aloud many times in his speeches, "What did I do to deserve this?" He is convinced that suffering is always a sign of wrongdoing. His reasoning seems to flow along the following lines, and it sounds very familiar to one who has listened attentively to suffering people. "If I do well, I will be blessed. If I sin I will be punished. If things are going badly, it must mean that there is something wrong with me morally and ethically. But I have searched and searched my heart, and find nothing condemnable there. Something is wrong. I deserve better than this. I ought to be immune to suffering since I have done nothing serious enough to deserve it. Or else there is sin somewhere in my past, some evil deed of which I am unaware; for this I am being punished. God, either show me my sin, or take away the punishment I am receiving undeservedly!"

There are Scriptures that clearly teach that sin will be visited in this life by suffering and hardship. There are passages in the Bible that teach the doctrine of divine chastisement for the purpose of refining and improving the character of the redeemed (e.g., Heb 12:7–13). But the story of Job indicates that there may be other reasons why hard things are to be found in the experience of even the best of God's people.

There is a truth here that says that our circumstances are not always a gauge of our spirituality. In this life we do not always get our desserts. The wicked sometimes prosper, right up to the grave. The righteous sometimes suffer severely, even to the end of their lives.

Are righteousness and godliness always rewarded in this life by prosperity and health? Some contemporary Bible teachers and evangelists would say yes. "We get what we deserve, or if we don't necessarily deserve it, we get what we ask for if we are people of faith." This idea is abroad in the Christian world today. There is a grain of truth in it. It is not totally heretical. But it needs the balance of the book of Job. "What did I do to deserve this?" he asked. The answer is, "Nothing." You did nothing to deserve all this ill treatment. But obviously you are not immune to it. It has come to you as it comes to many others, good and evil. Its coming can be explained, but in some cases, as in this case, not necessarily in terms of the sufferer's moral uprightness or lack of it.

Does prosperity always and inevitably follow the faithful? Do long life and good health always come to the one who lives by faith? Ask Job. Ask the Apostle Paul. Ask the martyrs of the ages. Ask the Lord Jesus Christ. The answer will come back, "Not always." This answer ought to be enough to warn us to stop asking always to receive our just desserts.[2]

---

2. Strahan neatly summarizes the theology of just desserts as Job and his friends would have held it: "The divine government accomplishes that which the best human government can only attempt—it rewards the deserving and punishes the guilty. The causal nexus between goodness and prosperity, sin and suffering, is never broken. Health, wealth, peace, comfort, long life are the lot of the true servants of God; sickness, poverty, trouble, disaster, early death the portion of the wicked. One's outward

As believers we know that we will not get what is coming to us. "For all have sinned and fall short of the glory of God" (Rom 3:23); "For the wages of sin is death, but the gift of God is eternal life in Christ Jesus our Lord" (Rom 6:23). Thank God. We will get what we certainly do not deserve: a place with the angels in the presence of the Father, forever and forever. In the meantime, we may suffer and suffer greatly. But St. Paul was granted a glimpse of what is ahead, and so was able to say (and I wish Job could have heard it and that we would believe it as fervently as Paul did), "I consider that our present sufferings are not worth comparing with the glory that shall be revealed in us" (Rom 8:18). Hear Paul's words in 2 Cor 4:16–18:

> Therefore we do not lose heart. Though outwardly we are wasting away, yet inwardly we are being renewed day by day. For our light and momentary troubles are achieving for us an eternal glory that far outweighs them all. So we fix our eyes not on what is seen, but on what is unseen. For what is seen is temporary, but what is unseen is eternal.

"Outwardly... inwardly..." My parishioner for many years, Miriam was a beautiful Christian woman. Her family loved her dearly and her church prized her involvement. Then cancer struck. Among other things, the disease took away her ability to speak. How well I remember the day we visited her hospital room, and when we arrived, her first words to us were hurriedly written on her Etch-a-Sketch board: "I'm growing stronger in the Lord every day!" The next time we visited, there was no strength to write. The next time, our dear friend was unrecognizable, just a small bundle of humanity rolled up in silence and pain. There was to be no next visit. Who won the victory in the life of this brave, good Christian? Cancer and disease did, surely. But in a far more profound sense, the winner was this child of God, who inwardly became stronger,

---

condition is always tell-tale, success being the indication of God's favor, failure of His anger. Accident and partiality are alike unknown. Famine, earthquake, pestilence, defeat in war are the punishment of sin; abundance of corn, wine, and oil, a peaceful home, and a numerous progeny, the reward of righteousness... The present life, rounded and complete in itself, alone counts for anything, and between the cradle and the grave men receive what they merit. A man's life and his lot in life must correspond, otherwise God would be unjust" (Strahan, *Book of Job*, 5). One objection to this theory, he says, is that "If prosperity was regarded as the evidence of God's favor, it is apparent that religion was still the possession of the rich, the free, the healthy, the happy, while it had no message for the poor, the broken, the defeated, the wretched" (Strahan, *Book of Job*, 6).

as the onslaught of suffering became ever more devastating. "Outwardly wasting away ... inwardly growing stronger every day."

"Light afflictions ... heavy weight of glory": Alfred Lewis was a dear man of God in one of my congregations. He was a farmer until age caught up with him and he had to sell all his land except a tiny corner on which he built a small house for himself and his wife. She became ill, and he spent several years until her death giving her his undivided and loving attention. Then ill health forced the sale of the little house, and Mr. Lewis moved into a senior's apartment. From the apartment he eventually had to move into a single room, then immobility drove him into bed permanently. As his pastor, I saw this dear man pass through these many stages of existence with dignity and courage. When we knew the end was near, we prayed together.

"Mr. Lewis, shall I pray that your life be extended?"

"No, Pastor. Pray that God will take me home. I'm ready, and there are those beyond waiting for me." So we prayed, and in the midst of his prayer, my dear friend ceased talking, and a strange and beautiful expression crossed his face. I knew he was seeing and hearing things that were invisible and inaudible to me. Then, in tones of sheer joy, he spoke.

"O Brother Dow, the Glory, the Glory, the Glory!"

This precious experience lasted only a moment. He resumed his prayer, and afterwards we said our farewells. The next morning Brother Lewis was gone; the place he had so obviously seen, the Glory he had glimpsed, was now the richer because my friend had gone home.

"Things seen ... things unseen": It was a bitterly cold winter night in Alberta. New to the province, I was riding in a very cold car along a country road headed for Edmonton. I noticed a sign in passing, "Bowden, 40 km." Then I saw some streetlights in the distance, almost clear enough to see their outline. "Where are those lights coming from," I asked my driver. "Why, those are the lights of Bowden," came the reply. I thought to myself, "Bowden? It can't be. We are forty kilometers from Bowden. Where I come from, nobody can see that far." Then I made the mistake of thinking out loud, and my friend at the wheel realized I didn't quite believe him. "These are the prairies," he said. "Out here nobody can be short-sighted." As women and men of faith, we can see what cannot otherwise be seen. We can see far into the distance, and sometimes, even when life brings few comforts, we can discern the lights of home. Does this help to make a sometimes very unpleasant journey endurable?

Reaction #5: "I'll never get over this!"

> Remember O God that my life is but a breath; my eyes will never see happiness again. (Job 7:7)

Never is a long time. How long did Job's trial last? We don't know. But we do know that he thought it would never come to an end. At least there were times when he felt this way. There are times when all suffering people feel this way. "The sun will never shine again!" they say. But Job's eyes did see happiness again. The trouble ended; the sun came out; the clouds disappeared.

Several years ago my first wife and I visited a church pastored by one of our young graduates. He and his wife had lost their first child just a couple of weeks before, and this was to be his first Sunday back in the pulpit. What would he say, and how would he ever get back into things again? We were moved and inspired by his faith-filled message that morning. It was entitled, "The Sun Always Rises." We went to comfort and encourage; we came away strengthened and inspired. This hope-filled message, related as it is to believers passing through storms, is included in the conclusion of this book.

When deeply hurting people say they will never recover, let's be gentle with them. They may not believe us when we assure them that "this, too, shall pass." Perhaps we should not even try to convince them that there might be light at the end of the tunnel. Perhaps it is enough to stand beside them with our love, hearing their words of near despair without judging them too harshly, all the time offering our presence and quiet understanding as tokens of our genuine friendship. Surely it is inappropriate to offer insensitive inanities in the fond hope of bringing cheer to someone whose heart is shattered.

As a pastor, I remember visiting an aged lady in hospital over a period of several weeks. She was near the gate of death. She knew it, I knew it, and there was no use pretending otherwise. As we became more comfortable talking about her coming journey, she indicated to me that she was not afraid, and wanted so much to talk about eternal life and heaven. Together we read passages about the bright hope of the believer and talked quietly and thoughtfully about them. She was a beautiful Christian, and longed to leave her body in which she had passed through so much illness and disease, and be at home with the Lord.

There was another lady in the same room who was also terminally ill, and who was suffering greatly. One day in the middle of my visit, the pastor of the other lady came to call. Our quiet meditation and precious conversation were suddenly interrupted by this man of the cloth singing lustily for the encouragement of his parishioner, "Pack up your troubles in your old kit bag, and smile, smile, smile!" I have never forgotten my feeling of distress. I was afraid this man lacked sensitivity in the presence of the most serious event facing a human being.

The words of Zophar to Job in 11:13–19 remind me of this incident involving what we might call cheerless cheer:

> Yet if you devote your heart to [God] and stretch out your hands to him, if you put away the sin that is in your hand and allow no evil to dwell in your tent, then you will lift up your face without shame; you will stand firm and without fear. You will surely forget your trouble, recalling it only as waters gone by. Life will be brighter than noonday, and darkness will become like morning. You will be secure, because there is hope; you will look about you and take your rest in safety. You will lie down with no one to make you afraid, and many will court your favor.

This may be good advice for some, perhaps. In context, however, the words seem to come too easily, and rhythmically the lilt seems altogether too frivolous.

Reaction #6: "Life makes no sense."

> I despise my life; I would not live forever. Let me alone; my days have no meaning. (Job 7:16)

Here Job asserts that life makes no sense. Again, it is difficult to criticize Job for believing this idea. So many senseless things had happened to him, for which there seemed to be no rhyme or reason. When all had been going well, life seemed to make beautiful sense. God was in his heaven, and all was well with the world. The righteous were blessed, the wicked were punished, justice and equity prevailed, and a perfect moral balance seemed operative in the world.

But with lightning speed Job's whole ordered universe was suddenly turned upside down. Gone were the old landmarks of meaning. Why all the years of toil, labor, struggle, achievement? It was all seemingly for nothing. There seemed to be no Grand Scheme left to believe in. And if no Grand Scheme, perhaps there was no Grand Architect, no Master Builder with a plan for each life and a plan for the whole.

All of us can identify with Job at this point. We have all, at one time or another, wondered if there is any ultimate meaning to life. Sometimes it all seems so piecemeal, so ragged-at-the-edges, so unlike the ordered design we describe in our teleological arguments for God's existence.

But in our better moments, we know our lives do have meaning. There is indeed a Grand Plan and we are a part of it. We may not know exactly how our part fits into the plot—we may sense only the action of the small scene in which we appear on the stage. Job, if your life had no meaning, then no one's has. What you did, how you responded, and the words you spoke, the faith you exhibited—who would dare say there is no meaning there, no significance to your struggles and the way you dealt with them? Why, we are convinced that you, Job, are one of the most important characters ever to step out of the wings and into the action of human existence.

Does it mean anything to prove that Satan does not have ultimate power over God's servants? Does it mean anything to see the Prince of the Power of the Air defeated by a mere mortal, determined to stay true to his God and his convictions? Is there any meaning in faith triumphing over despair, hope conquering doubt and dismal fainting? "My days have no meaning," you say? You know not of what you speak. We know better, Job. And perhaps because you raised this question, and we have pondered it in the light of the significance of your life and witness to the ages, we will each be a little more assured of our own unique significance in the plan of God, which will keep unfolding down to the horizon of eternity. When tempted to utter the words, "My life makes no sense," we will remember you, and the temptation will be resisted.

Reaction #7: "O God, leave me alone!"

> Will you never look away from me, or let me alone even for an instant? (Job 7:19)

The pain persists. Physical agony will not go away, and heartache is almost unbearable. Job cries out, "O God, leave me alone!" The sentiment is echoed again in Job 10:20, "Turn away from me so I can have a moment's joy." How sad that Job thought of God as his tormenter! God was his Master, and the one who thought so highly of his servant. Even now, the Almighty was keeping himself in check, watching his servant achieve victory in the arena of agony. And Job, who at times longed for God with an intolerable longing, now calls upon him to depart, to look away, to busy himself with some other more important cosmic business. How sad that we, too, sometimes misunderstand God's gracious dealings with us, and wish he were a little less omnipresent.

A friend told me how one day he came upon his grandson whose hand was in the cookie jar. "Grandpa, don't look!" he said. And so we say to God when we step from the path, "Father, don't look!" Or, weary with heartache, and blaming God for our woes, we wish him to stop tormenting us: "O God, just leave me alone!"

Do we really mean it? If God should ever abandon us, where would we be? Job, you are not abandoned. Neither are you the object of God's whimsical malice. We cannot explain that to you; but we can assure ourselves of these truths: your story is an invaluable aid in our understanding of God and his ways with us.

Reaction #8: "What's the use? If God is against me, what chance do I have?"

> His wisdom is profound, his power is vast . . . He alone stretches out the heavens and treads on the waves of the sea. He is the Maker of the Bear and Orion, the Pleiades and the constellations of the south. He performs wonders that cannot be fathomed, miracles that cannot be numbered." (Job 9:4–10)

Job speaks of God's inscrutable activity in his own life:

> How then can I dispute with him? How can I find words to argue with him? Though I were innocent, I could not answer him; I could only plead with my Judge for mercy. Even if I summoned him and he responded, I do not believe he would give me a hearing. He would crush me with a storm and multiply my wounds for no reason. He would not let me regain my breath but would overwhelm me with misery. If it is a matter of strength, he is mighty! If it is a matter of justice, who will summon him? Even if I were innocent my mouth would condemn me; if I were blameless, it would pronounce me guilty. Although I am blameless, I have no concern for myself; I despise my own life. It is all the same; that is why I say, "He destroys both the blameless and the wicked." When a scourge brings sudden death, he mocks the despair of the innocent. When a land falls into the hand of the wicked, he blindfolds its judges. If it is not he, then who is it? (Job 9:14–24)

There's no use arguing with his omnipotence. I'm at the mercy of One infinitely more powerful than I am. God's sovereignty is destroying me, and there is nothing I can do about it. Job 9 is an important chapter for conveying to the reader the essence of Job's doctrine of God. The greatness and majesty of the all-powerful God are revealed in every statement. Yet, Job is troubled.

God is infinitely great, and absolutely sovereign. That means, to Job, that everything that happens comes directly from God's hand. If evil comes to one not deserving it, this can only mean that Job has been wrong, not about the might of God, but about the character of God. Job is greatly confused. He concludes that God is the author of the evil that befalls us as well as of the good. His purposes are all inscrutable. There is no use asking why things happen; one can only surrender in hopeless resignation to the activity of a God whose system of justice is at odds with human reason. The ways of God, seemingly grossly unfair, are unfathomable. Why seek answers? Why continue to endure in hope? The reaction: "What's the use?"

"If it is not he, then who is it?" This is surely one of the most significant questions asked by Job. "If it is not God who is responsible for all that has happened to me, then who is?" Again, we wish it were possible to dialogue personally with Job. We know that Satan would have to come into the conversation. We would correct Job as he has come to believe in God's responsibility for the evil that has befallen him. God is not an unapproachable despot who whimsically and maliciously brings about the downfall of the innocent. He is a God of righteousness and justice and mercy. He hears your words, Job.

Similarly, he hears our words as well. How our words spoken in ignorance and misunderstanding must wound the heart of him who loves us and longs to deliver us from evil, and who will so deliver us eternally as our trust, confidence and faith are securely fixed upon him. Job's ignorance of the ways of God in the world and with himself is responsible for this outburst of insult. Because he is ignorant, and because he is on the ash heap of agony, we forgive these words. But we will not accept them as anything but the ravings of a pathetic sufferer. The very book in which these words are uttered tells us they are simply not true. They are the reactions of many similarly afflicted agonizers, however, and we need to listen to them and take the plight they represent very seriously.

Reaction #9: "O, that there were someone to come between God and me, someone to speak to God on my behalf!"

> [God] is not a man like me that I might answer him, that we might confront each other in court. If only there were someone to arbitrate between us, to lay his hand upon us both, someone to remove God's rod from me, so that his terror would frighten me no more. Then I would speak up without fear of him, but as it now stands with me, I cannot. (Job 9:32–35)

How we long to share with Job the fact and the wonder of the Incarnation. How much we should like to tell him of Jesus, who came into the world to be the mediator between God and humanity for whom Job longed. Christ *is* the arbitrator, the Peacemaker, the Conciliator, the Reconciler of a Holy God with sinful people. He does lay his hand upon both the Father and the sinner: "Therefore since we have been justified through faith we *have* peace with God through our Lord Jesus Christ" (Rom 5:1). He has removed God's rod from us: "The Lord has laid on him the iniquity of us all" (Isa 53:6). We can speak up without fear in his presence:

> Therefore, since we have a great high priest who has gone through the heavens, Jesus the Son of God, let us hold firmly to the faith we profess. For we do not have a high priest who is unable to sympathize with our weaknesses, but we have one who has been tempted in every way, just as we are—yet was without sin. Let us then approach the throne of grace with confidence, so that we may receive mercy and find grace to help us in our time of need." (Heb 4:14–16)

Job was a great man; one of the greatest persons ever to live before the time of Christ. We have God's word on that. But he did live before Christ. His words are filled with the longing of those living in ancient times for more light, more hope, more revelation from God, who spoke in those days by the prophets, but has "in these last days spoken unto us by his Son" (Heb.1:2). Humbly and thankfully we ought to be grateful for the light of the gospel.

Reaction #10: "God is the author of misfortune and disaster"

> To God belong wisdom and power; counsel and understanding are his. What he tears down cannot be rebuilt; the man he imprisons cannot be released. If he holds back the waters, there is drought; if he lets them loose they devastate the land . . . He leads

> counselors away stripped and makes fools of judges ... He leads priests away stripped and overthrows men long established. He silences the lips of trusted advisers and takes away the discernment of elders. He pours contempt on nobles and disarms the mighty. He reveals the deep things of darkness and brings deep shadows into the light. He makes nations great, and destroys them; he enlarges nations, and disperses them. He deprives the leaders of the earth of their reason; he sends them wandering through a trackless waste. They grope in darkness with no light; he makes them stagger like drunkards. (Job 12:13–25)

In chapter 12, Job claims that God's sovereign might produces only disaster and misfortune. His concept of God's character is being shaped drastically by his own circumstances. The charge he lays is that God is, above all else, the author of misfortune and disaster. Note in the progression of his thinking the ascription of evil intent to God's mighty acts in Job 12:13–25.

Job has been beset by one devastating hardship after another. His theological reflections are bound to be conditioned by his recent calamities and present misery. Surely Job's view of God has become warped, twisted by his own view of the world. Job knows better. He will yet speak more positively of the Almighty, whom he has known intimately in brighter times. We must forgive him for uttering foolish sentiments even about the character of God. When his situation improves, his theology will likewise become more positive. Job, the God you (and many who speak like you) describe in this passage is more akin to a devil. This is not the God and Father of our Lord Jesus Christ. "O Lord, help us to remember this, when we are in the throes of agony, and are tempted to lash out at you with concepts bordering on blasphemy." God, as he is revealed in the Bible, does not change. He does not suffer alteration when the concepts people have of him are altered. We have the Scriptures as an unchanging standard to guide us in our understanding of the nature, personality and purposes of God! People's concepts may be conditioned by circumstance but Jesus Christ is the same yesterday, today, and forever.

Reaction #11: "Life is a game, and the game is fixed!"

> Man's days are determined; you have decreed the number of his months and have set limits he cannot exceed. So look away from him and let him alone, till he has put in his time like a hired man. (Job 14:5–6)

Job briefly comes into possession of a theology of absolute determinism. He begins to feel like a puppet on a string, at the mercy of forces far beyond his control or understanding. Carried to its logical end, this view of life is most disheartening. We are but pawns, playing-pieces in the hands of one involved in a mere game. Helpless, we are moved about the board, perhaps to protect a more important piece, and when necessary, sacrificed and cast aside. The game is the thing, the pieces totally uninvolved in the choices that determine their individual destinies.

Job, you are wrong. You have the game in your hands. The choices you make to remain steadfast in you confidence in God and in righteousness will determine the outcome of this contest. Your will, your determination, are what matter most. The game is not fixed; the end is up to you! And, we know, to us. We believe that our choices matter to God. Our humanity is legitimate, we are responsible and free under God to determine to obey or disobey, to persevere or to give up. Divine sovereignty has granted to us a measure of human sovereignty. In fact it is the book of Job that illustrates this truth. Although Job does not know it, God is trusting him to make the right choices—will he endure without having his questions satisfactorily answered, or will he not? The outcome hangs in the balance. It is Job's responsibility to live up to God's expectations of him as his long-time friend and servant. His relationship with God has made him the man he is. Will chaotic circumstances cause Job to become something other than he has been, or will he remain God's friend and servant whatever happens? Job chooses the latter course of action, and for this we honor him.

A caution is in order here. In a sense our dialogues with Job do him disservice. They might be construed as suggesting our superiority to Job, because we know more than he did. In fact, in spite of his questions, Job did persevere. His story is remarkable quite without any reference to New Testament teaching. Job in the context of the Hebrew Scriptures and Wisdom tradition in particular, stands on its own as a remarkable story of the victory of a human who chose God and righteous living when to do otherwise would have seemed the most sensible thing to do. The story of Job (like all Old Testament stories), is not in the Bible merely to give us the opportunity to demean it by comparison to New Testament understanding.

Reaction #12: "Life is sheer misery, then you die!"

Job begins the fourteenth chapter with words that still appear in funeral Scripture readings:

> Man born of woman is of few days and full of trouble. He springs up like a flower and withers away; like a fleeting shadow, he does not endure. (Job 14:1–2)

Listen to the intense sadness in his words in the middle of this speech:

> At least there is hope for a tree: If it is cut down, it will sprout again, and its new shoots will not fail. Its roots may grow old in the ground and its stump die in the soil, yet at the scent of water it will bud and put forth shoots like a plant. But man dies and is laid low; he breathes his last and is no more. As water disappears from the sea or a river bed becomes parched and dry, so man lies down and does not rise; till the heavens are no more, men will not awake or be roused from their sleep. (Job 14:7–12)

And the end of the chapter has a pall of gloom spread over all of life:

> But as a mountain erodes and crumbles and as a rock is moved from its place, as water wears away stones and torrents wash away the soil, so you [God] destroy man's hope. You overpower him once for all, and he is gone; you change his countenance and send him away. If his sons are honored, he does not know it; if they are brought low, he does not see it. He feels but the pain of his own body and mourns only for himself. (Job 14:18–22)

Here is the reaction of deep discouragement bordering on utter despair.

We could argue with Job, of course, and insist that his words are colored by his circumstances, that he is exaggerating and overstating the bleakness of living and the hopelessness of dying. But perhaps we would do better to merely listen and sympathize with the heartbroken cries coming from this stricken human being. Go ahead and weep, Job. Your tears and your melancholy assessment of life as you see it are altogether justified. We will not even say, "We understand. We know how you must feel." We do not know. We have not lost so much or suffered so much. In the face of such grief we can only silently ache with this terribly hurting soul.

Would we dare say, "Cheer up, Job! Count it all joy when you suffer so. Give God thanks for everything that has happened to you. When you begin to praise the Lord, your fortunes will improve"? I include these words here because they are representative of a popular approach to suffering among believers. But when applied to the woebegone Job at this point in the book, do they not appear out-of-place and inappropriate? The importance of praise-filled living is stressed in the New Testament. The belief that trials provide opportunity for personal growth is certainly taught by the apostle Paul. We must not press these ideas, as important and valuable as they are, beyond the intent of the Scriptures, however. In Gethsemane there are tears, and they are precious tears. Jesus was a man of joy. He told the disciples that he had spoken to them so that his joy might be in them, and their joy might be full (John 15:11). Many times Jesus said to his friends, "Be of good cheer!" He is also remembered, however, as the Man of Sorrows, the one acquainted with grief.

Is this a contradiction—Man of Joy, Man of Sorrows? Or is it a fact that there was in Jesus that perfection of personality in which the ability to respond appropriately to life allowed for joyous times and times of bitter lamentation? Jesus wept at the grave of Lazarus. We love him for those tears. They tell us that he does understand our sorrows, he does identify with our grief, he possesses feelings just like ours; and he is able, as no one else, not only to understand us, but to help us. His tears seemed to have been tears of sadness for the sorrow of his friends at the loss of their brother. His agonies in Gethsemane derived from the inner conflict when facing the pain of becoming the world's sin bearer.

There was joy for Jesus, says the writer of Hebrews, but it was for the "joy set before Him"—future joy, the joy that follows the suffering and agony that he endured. For this joy Jesus endured the cross. He did not enjoy it, although, remarkably he did give thanks for it at the Last Supper just as we thanks for that suffering at every Communion service. He *endured* the cross (Heb 12:2). As with Jesus, so with Job, and so with all of us as believers when called upon to suffer: in endurance there is victory.

Reaction #13: "Life just isn't fair."

> God has wronged me and drawn his net around me. Though I cry, "I've been wronged!" I get no response; though I call for help, there is no justice. (Job 19:6–7)

Job has become convinced that God is punishing him without proper cause. Multitudes have uttered sentiments such as this as they have suffered illness or reverses of one kind or another. Many times we hear it said, as onlookers observe undeserving persons being called upon to suffer loss, "There's no justice. It just isn't fair!"

People work for years and years to raise, educate, and help establish their children for life. Retirement time approaches. Mortgages are all paid; financial security is at last a reality. The opportunity to really begin to enjoy life without worry or necessary labor is finally almost at hand. Then it happens. Serious illness, perhaps even death come to visit and the opportunity is gone—forever.

I recall a couple I had known since I was a child. After years of living in rented apartments and small houses, Margaret and Al finally had enough money to purchase their own home and decorate it just the way they desired. The last thing they designed and had installed in their dream cottage was a beautiful set of kitchen cabinets. The cupboards lined one whole wall of the kitchen, and how proud Margaret was of them! I sat at the kitchen table admiring them, and Margaret was so proud and so happy!

Not long at all after that, Al became ill, and was diagnosed with brain cancer. He failed very quickly, and within weeks passed away. Unbelievably, a few weeks after his death, his wife was diagnosed as having the same dread disease. Margaret entered hospital, suffered terribly, and died before she was fifty years old, and, needless to say, before she could really enjoy her home and her wonderful cupboards. On the day I conducted her funeral, I remember hearing many people in the funeral home and in the reception following express words similar to those spoken here by Job: "There is no justice! It all seems so unfair."

It is quite amazing that these speeches of Job have been preserved for us in the Bible. Here is a man expressing for the entire world to hear his conviction that injustice is the lot of humanity, and that the way God deals with people is unfair. The person expressing these thoughts is not a skeptical unbeliever, or an out-and-out atheist. It is God's servant, the one God praises, who speaks these very human yet very disturbing words.

Is the idea that Job expresses, and many in the world repeat, is this notion that "there is no justice" true or false?

In part the idea is true. Unfair things do happen to people. The story of Margaret and her cupboards is but one of a multitude of stories, many of them with far more serious implications, that could be told to substantiate the notion that life is very unfair to many people a great deal of the time. It would be wrong, however, to overstate the case, and say that life is always unfair, or even that it is unfair most of the time to all people or even to most people. Much of life for many people is pleasant and enjoyable. Job is speaking from the ash heap of absolute desolation. His words must be understood as coming from a man near the brink of despair.

Having said that, we still ask, why is life often unfair? The Bible gives an answer that is not acceptable to many, but that offers to the one who accepts it a measure of understanding. The Bible asserts that the world in which we live is a fallen world. It is a world out of joint, out of order to a large degree, not at all the perfect world originally created by God.

The fall of humanity and the consequent curse upon creation are terribly important doctrines that, when taken seriously and accepted literally, offer an explanation to help our perplexity with regard to injustices as humans experience them.

In this world under the curse, there are many unfair things to be observed in the lives of others and experienced personally. Often, as Job observed, and as the psalmist reiterated, the wicked seem to prosper and the righteous suffer. This is certainly Job's complaint in Job 21:23–33:

> One man dies in full vigor, completely secure and at ease, his body well nourished, his bones rich with marrow. Another man dies in bitterness of soul, never having enjoyed anything good. Side by side they lie in the dust, and worms cover them both . . . the evil man is spared from the day of calamity . . . he is delivered from the day of wrath. Who denounces his conduct to his face? Who repays him for what he has done? He is carried to the grave, and watch is kept over his tomb. The soil in the valley is sweet to him; all men follow after him, and a countless throng goes before him.

Job summarizes the injustice of the problem-free life of the wicked in Job 21:7–15:

> Why do the wicked live on, growing old and increasing in power? They see their children established around them, their offspring before their eyes. Their homes are safe and free from fear; the rod of God is not upon them. Their bulls never fail to breed; their cows calve and do not miscarry. They send forth their children as a flock; their little ones dance about. They sing to the music of the tambourine and harp; they make merry to the sound of the flute. They spend their years in prosperity and go down to the grave in peace. Yet they say to God, "Leave us alone! We have no desire to

know your ways. Who is the Almighty that we should serve him? What would we gain by praying to him?"

In chapter 24 Job describes the injustice of the oppression of the poor (of whom Job has great knowledge and for whom he has great compassion), and God's seeming indifference to it:

> Men move boundary stones; they pasture flocks they have stolen. They drive away the orphan's donkey and take the widow's ox in pledge. They thrust the needy from the path and force all the poor of the land into hiding. Like wild donkeys in the desert, the poor go about their labor of foraging food; the wasteland provides food for their children. They gather fodder in the fields and glean in the vineyards of the wicked. Lacking clothes, they spend the night naked; they have nothing to cover themselves in the cold ... The groans of the dying rise from the city, and the souls of the wounded cry out for help. But God charges no one with wrongdoing. (Job 24:2–7, 12)

There *is* injustice in the world. It does not seem fair that some live far from God and yet prosper, and some live close to God and suffer intensely. "In the beginning it was not so," but in the present, this is the world we live in. It is not "the best of all possible worlds," for God created the world and pronounced it originally "good." Nor is it the world as it will always be, for there is coming a day when the former things will pass away, and there will be a new heaven and a new earth, "the home of righteousness" (2 Pet 3:13). We live between the original good world, and the final perfect world. And Paul indicates that in this "meantime" era, all creation is groaning as it suffers the pains of its dissolution and awaits its redemption that is sure to come. (Rom 8:20–22).

Nor has this fallen, cursed, lost world, where unfairness seems so often to rule, been abandoned by God. The story of the Bible is the story of God's unwearying discontent with the status quo. God has been at work since the fall to put things right, and not the least of his work has been the work of redemption. Christ came into the world to deal with the fall, and the curse, and to restore righteousness, justice, and fairness to human existence. Those who know Christ, know that many things happened to him that were unjust and unfair. But we also know that because of his life, death, resurrection, and ascension victory, there is coming a day when all wrongs will be righted, all injustice done away with forever. Beginning on that day no one will ever say again, "there is no justice; it just isn't fair." We remind ourselves that all God's accounts are not settled in the here and now. Though Job recognized it but dimly, there is an eternal world, and in that realm judgment and justice will be applied fairly and equitably. "Will not the Judge of all the earth do right?" said Abraham (Gen 18:25).

Job errs in equating life with God. To say that life is unfair is not tantamount to saying that God is unfair. In a limited sense, Satan is the Prince of this world. He has some power over the affairs of men. Inequity, injustice, iniquity—he is their source and inspiration. Satan's sovereignty, however, is limited by God's absolute will. This limited sovereignty is exercised at great human cost.

But he who is absolute is winning the battle. The conflict of the ages rages even now; the decisive battle in this warfare was waged on the Cross. Those who follow Christ follow him to ultimate victory. "Thanks be to God," said the apostle Paul, "who always leads us in a triumphal procession in Christ!" (2 Cor 2:14). In Christ we have victory in life and over life, even if life is filled with pain and sorrow. Victory in death and over death, even pain-filled, agonizing, disease-ridden death, is ours through our Redeemer.

In the lives of believers and unbelievers alike, periods of injustice and unfairness may occur. But the believer knows that ultimate victory does not belong to these activities of Satan. We are still in the world; we are not in heaven yet. Here we may suffer in a measure like Job. Our faith and hope, however, are in him who is Victor. "More than conquerors"—that name belongs to those who belong to Christ.

Reaction #14: "Have pity on me."

> [God] has alienated my brothers from me; my acquaintances are completely estranged from me. My kinsmen have gone away; my friends have forgotten me ... My breath is offensive to my wife; I am loathsome to my own brothers. Even the little boys scorn me; when I appear, they ridicule me. All my intimate friends detest me; those I love have turned against me. I am nothing but skin and bones; I have escaped with only the skin of my teeth. Have pity upon me, my friends, have pity, for the hand of God has struck me. (Job 19:13–21)

In chapter 19, Job pleads for pity from his friends. He speaks with obvious horror of his physical deterioration. "Look at me, and be astonished," he pleads (Job 21:5). "Do something to indicate you understand the horrible nightmare through which I am passing."

These must surely be among the saddest words in the literature of the human race. Yet if we had ears to hear, they could be heard as a chorus in the hospitals of our land. They are the expressed thoughts of many of the aged, the infirm, those suffering from terrible debilitating and often terminal illnesses. I recall working as an attendant in a hospital for people suffering with chronic illness. One patient had a dreadful disease that had eaten away his lower jaw. Otherwise he seemed almost normal. But his appearance when dressings were removed was unbelievably frightening, and the smell unbearable. None of us on staff wanted to be assigned to his care. I cannot recall that he ever had visitors. Undoubtedly, he had been a person with dignity, honor, and friends. But he was reduced to an isolated individual that everyone avoided.

For one who has known good health and robust physical wellness to be clasped in the jaws of an illness that is irreversible in its devastating power, life can become an excruciatingly agonizing misery. These words of Job seem to be spoken in a mood of almost breathless panic. "Look at what is happening to me. Can you believe the damage the diseases I suffer have done to me! I hardly recognize myself; and moment-by-moment things are getting terribly worse. O, friends, help me if you can. Pity me if you cannot. God is out to destroy and there is nothing that can stop his onslaughts!"

Job refers to his physical anguish in others passages, such as this one in Job 30:27–31:

> The churning inside me never stops; days of suffering confront me. I go about blackened, but not by the sun ... I have become a brother of jackals, a companion of owls. My skin grows black and peels; my body burns with fever. My harp is tuned to mourning, and my flute to the sound of wailing.

Listen to his plaintive wail in Job 7:2–7:

> Like a slave longing for the evening shadows, or a hired man waiting eagerly for his wages, so I have been allotted months of futility, and nights of misery have been assigned to me. When I lie down I think, "How long before I get up?" The night drags on, and I toss till dawn. My body is clothed with worms and scabs; my skin is broken and festering. My days are swifter than a weaver's shuttle, and they come to an end without hope. Remember,

> O God, that my life is but a breath; my eyes will never see happiness again.

In some ways it might be said that the book of Job is a case study in suffering. Job is a classic case of a person who undergoes as much as any human being could ever be expected to endure. He is God's servant, but he is a human being; he is a person. When we listen to him, we can, if we will, hear the voice of a multitude of suffering people. We can ponder his words and meditate upon them until we feel our way into his situation. We can ache with Job, weep with him, listen to his moaning, and in our listening we can learn. We can learn what it means to be human and to be hurting. We can, if we will, develop a heart for the agonizing of the world's people, and if we are very careful we can learn to speak comfort to their deepest hurts.

What happens to people when they undergo intense pain? How do they think? How do they articulate their deepest feelings? Can we get inside the skin of a person in the grip of genuine agony, so that we can understand her at least in some small measure? If we can understand him, and hear her, we may be better able to understand other sufferers. We may grow in our sympathy, in our sensitivity. Our responses to sufferers and to suffering itself will demonstrate the fruit of this growth. Reading, rereading, analyzing, and empathetically reflecting on Job's words, I believe, can make more humane and understanding people out of us. This will only happen if we listen, and do not yield to the temptation, as Job's three friends did, to jump to immediate conclusions with explanation, interpretation, and judgmental diagnosis.

Reaction #15: "O God, where are you?"

> Even today my complaint is bitter; his hand is heavy in spite of my groaning. If only I knew where to find him; if only I could go to his dwelling! I would state my case before him and fill my mouth with arguments. I would find out what he would answer me, and consider what he would say ... But if I go to the east he is not there; if I go to the west, I do not find him. When he is at work in the north I do not see him; when he turns to the south, I catch no glimpse of him ... But he stands alone, and who can oppose him? He does whatever he pleases. He carries out his decree against me, and many such plans he still has in store. That is why I am terrified before him; when I think of all this, I fear him. (Job 23:2–9, 13–15)

The words of the twenty-third chapter sum up Job's pathetic longing for a vision of God, or even for the sound of the voice of God. Although he refuses to believe it, there seems to be no one out there in the void, no voice to break the cosmic silence of meaninglessness.

At times, we have noted, Job wishes that God would depart from him, and leave him alone. Here he longs for God with an incredible aching thirst. Had Job been an atheist, his situation would have been in a sense more bearable. At least he would have been able to say, "There is no God. There is only blind fate, and fate is impersonal. Life cannot be expected to be orderly or meaningful. What comes must be accepted without question, because there is no scheme of meaning to which individual events can be attached. There is no universal scheme—just multitudes of unrelated particulars, none of which can be expected to divulge meaning as to the whole of existence. With resignation I must take what comes." This is not a very positive world-view, to be sure, but at least it relieves the pressure that a person goes through who expects life to have form, structure, meaning, purpose, and direction, and who discovers, despairingly, that apparently there are times when it does not.

Job is not an atheist, however. He cannot cease believing in God and fearing God. If God is, then there must be a reason for all events in life. The thinking believer wants to be able to discern the providential hand of God in everything. Nehemiah was convinced of the good hand of God upon his enterprise. Surely it would be good if Job could see God at work in his troubled situation. Would it be too much to expect that now and then God would reveal himself, or at least speak words of consolation from heaven to soothe the mind of his troubled servant? But no revelation is forthcoming. And for so long, the voice of God is silent. God's apparent abandonment of his servant is to Job the greatest of all his misfortunes.[3]

Just when he is most needed, it seems, God chooses to disappear. Job seems to suggest that if only God would show himself, if only his existence could be verified for an instant, if only one could be sure he was still there . . . if only. To this sensitive believing servant of God, the greatest agony of all is the total absence of any indication of God's existence

---

3. Rohr, *Job and the Mystery of Suffering*, 47, writes, "The Paradox of the Book of Job is that Yahweh remains totally present in power, yet to all appearances does nothing. And for thirty-seven chapters God says nothing. It is our [certainly Job's] worst nightmare: a silent, hidden and ineffective God."

and presence. It is strange, but seems to be the case, that a sense of God's presence is sometimes absent in the midst of the severest of human trials. Our major piece of evidence for this assertion comes from the lips of the Savior himself, in the moment of his greatest agony. "My God, My God," he cried on the cross, "why have you forsaken me?"

It is sometimes suggested that pain draws us to God and suffering makes us more aware of his nearness.[4] Listen to Rohr speak of the value of suffering to Job: "God can set us right only by breaking us down. As long as we remain in a self-assured, righteous, left-brain position, there is no way we can be bridge builders or reconcilers. We are going to see in Job how God breaks this man down so he can enter into a newer and better definition of truth, a better understanding of how God creates life on earth."[5] Perhaps some have found this to be so. Job and Jesus apparently did not. Intense pain and acute illnesses make people aware of pain's presence, not of God's. Perhaps the reason some have sensed God at such times is because they have consciously determined to believe in his nearness and afterwards took that determination to be the thing itself.

There is a philosophy of pain that ascribes to it more beneficial and therapeutic qualities than it possesses. Pain is good, illness is a blessing, it is asserted. "Being put on my back by God was the best thing that ever happened to me. God spoke to me in my illness. I am a better person because of the suffering inflicted upon me." We have all heard people testify in this way. To some these sentiments are helpful. To others they may seem to be patent nonsense. In the midst of agony, one is often totally taken up with survival. God, sometimes at least, seems to be the last thing one cares to consider or is indeed able to consider.[6]

---

4. Tabb, *Whirlwind*, 195, says, "When we find the world too much of a distraction to keep us from seeing God, he breaks its hold on us through trouble. We treat God like a life-jacket in our fishing boat, so God lets our boat spring a leak in the middle of Lake Superior ... And he will continue to use the bad things of life to draw us closer to himself ... as long as life endures ... If bad times never came, we would never develop true intimacy with God. Our relationship would never progress." How this applies to Job is not made clear, unless we assume that Tabb is convinced Job needs trouble to improve his relationship with God, which I have taken pains to demonstrate is not the case.

5. Rohr, *Job and the Mystery of Suffering*, 44. Yet Rohr has just said "[Job's] troubles don't make Job into a saint. They confirm the goodness already there" (p. 32).

6. Even so helpful a scholarly work as Harrison's *Introduction to the Old Testament*, takes this "pain is valuable" philosophy seriously, and erroneously concludes, "One of the great merits of the book [of Job] is its insistence that the experience of suffering,

Could it be that pain was never intended to bring us to God? Could it be that in some cases at least, its sole function is to preoccupy the sufferer so that God seems to be far away, and getting farther away all the time? Let these words of Job convince us that the suffering human being must sometimes wait out periods of apparent forsakenness and abandonment. And the waiting can be absolute agony.

PSALM 22 AND JOB: FROM DEEPEST DARKNESS TO THE BRIGHTNESS OF MORNING

The important words in this train of thought are "sometimes" and "apparent," for of course the believer is never really forsaken, any more than Job was, any more than Jesus was upon the cross. Reflecting upon Psalm 22, the Psalm that begins with the words, "My God, my God, why . . ." may help us in our thinking here. The psalm title is "to the doe of the morning," or poetically, it is thought, "the first light after the darkness of the night."

The psalm begins with a sensation of abandonment by God, and it is quite possible that Jesus was beginning to recite the whole psalm when he uttered the first words of it on Calvary. The psalm is an amazing prophecy of what eventually transpired on Golgotha. We have God's servant surrounded by angry onlookers who mock him, taunt him, and gamble for his garments. We have described for us his agony as his hands

---

in one form or another, is necessary for spiritual maturity" (p. 1045). Or consider the explanation of Archer, *Survey of Old Testament Introduction*, 454, "This book [Job] deals with the theoretical problem of pain in the life of the godly. It undertakes to answer the question, Why do the righteous suffer? This answer comes in a threefold form: (1) God is worthy of love even apart from the blessings He bestows; (2) God may permit suffering as a means of purifying and strengthening the soul in godliness; (3) God's thoughts and ways are moved by considerations too vast for the puny mind of man to comprehend, since man is unable to see the issues of life with the breadth and vision of the Almighty; nevertheless God really knows what is best for His own glory and for our ultimate good." It is the position taken by answer (2) against which I have argued repeatedly in these pages. The answer may be true in general, but is definitely not a conclusion derived from a study of Job. Author-lecturer Joyce Landorf, who suffered greatly with the pain of temperomandibular joint dysfunction, says realistically: "There is a certain amount of head knowledge within me that says someday the Lord, in His mercy, will step in and stop this hideous round of pain, which is attacking on a never-ending basis. Isn't that what a loving heavenly Father would do? Yet here, in my heart, I cannot see, touch, or feel God; and the silence of my life is deadly. God seems to be doing nothing—nothing at all" (Landorf, *Silent September*, 7). Like Job, she found this function of pain incomprehensible, yet actual.

and feet were pierced, as his thirst became so great, and as he knew he was on the verge of death. Notice verses 6 and 7: "But I am a worm and not a man, scorned by men and despised by the people. All who see me mock me; they hurl insults, shaking their heads: 'He trusts in the Lord; let the Lord rescue him. Let him deliver him, since he delights in him.'" No one can read this psalm, written hundreds of years before the crucifixion, and fail to be amazed at the correlation between the words of David and the events of Calvary.

The psalm does not end on the negative note of suffering and shame, however. The mood of the poem suddenly shifts from gloom to brightness in the nineteenth verse. The first shafts of morning light begin to appear on the horizon. One is soon able to see clearly the outlines of the doe of the morning, the first object to be seen on what promises to be a bright and beautiful day. Notice, for example, verses 23–31, and imagine these words coming from the lips of Jesus the Savior, who is able, even in the darkest hour, to see something of "the joy that was set before him."

> You who fear the Lord, praise him! All you descendants of Jacob, honor him! Revere him, all you descendants of Israel! For he has not despised or disdained the suffering of the afflicted one; he has not hidden his face from him but has listened to his cry for help." (Ps 22:23–24)

These are the words of a new dawn. They are brave, hopeful, victory-oriented words. They remind us that in the experience of Jesus, the sense of being abandoned by God did not last. Before he died, he was abundantly certain that God had heard his cry, and had come to his rescue. Are these not also words that Job might have uttered after the night of his misery, and in the full light of the dawn of the peaceful day described in the epilogue of his story?

The last words of Psalm 22 are a world away from being words of dejection and desolation. Verses 27–31 read,

> All the ends of the earth will remember [the story of the cross? 'This do in remembrance of me'] and turn to the Lord, and all the families of the nations will bow down before him, for dominion belongs to the Lord and he rules over the nations... Posterity will serve him; future generations will be told about the Lord. They will proclaim his righteousness to a people yet unborn—for he has done it.

If, as I have suggested, Jesus recited this psalm on the cross and saw so much of its prophecy being fulfilled before his eyes, then the last words of the psalm may well have been the last words or thoughts of the suffering Savior. These are the words of one who is able to see down the corridors of history and tell of people throughout the whole world calling on God and serving him in righteousness, all because the suffering was endured, and a great victory for humanity was thereby secured. "For he [who said on Calvary, 'It is finished!'] *has* done it!" Jesus endured the dark night of pain and endured the sense of abandonment by his beloved Father. He lived to see the bright new dawn, and all who know him share in that brightness.

And Job, who said, "O God, where are you?" endured the darkness and desolation too; then he could say, "I am unworthy—how can I reply to you? I put my hand over my mouth" (Job 40:4) and "My ears had heard of you but now my eyes have seen you" (Job 42:5). The best thing to do with pain is to endure it. The best thing to do with sickness, disease, grief, or sorrow is not to try to befriend them as though they have come to visit as live-in tutors sharing the secrets of their knowledge; no, the thing to do is endure, and to believe that as surely as morning follows night, the doe of the morning will be visible at last.

How well I remember the period of awful grieving following the death of my first wife, Carolyn. Wise counsel advised me to face into the darkness and stay there as long as it took. Months of depression and near despair followed. But simply waiting in the dark, trying to pray, and enduring this awful cross, seeking to hang on until morning, which seemed as though it would never come—well, the dawn is at last beginning to break.

SUMMARY

The preceding pages have been an attempt to analyze some of the very human, and largely negative reactions of Job the suffering servant of God. In the next section, the more positive reactions of Job, the person of faith will be considered. This is not to suggest that we have exhausted the list of questioning human responses to suffering depicted in the speeches of Job, however. Ideas suggested in the speeches do overlap, and I have tried to avoid undue repetition in the discussion. We might have spent some time considering reactions like "Why me?" (Job 10:18), or "Nobody understands what I'm going through" (Job 13:5–11), or even,

"O for the good old days" (Job 29). I hope that enough material has been covered to demonstrate what an amazing book Job is in the universality and timelessness of its discussion of the whole issue of human woe.

The great value of the book, however, goes beyond its depiction of the humanness of its chief character, as important as this concept is. God's servant is human, nevertheless, and his words demonstrate over and over that, like Elijah, he was a person like us. But Job was above all a person of faith. Throughout the speeches there are flashes of faith-filled insight that drive Job on in his determination not to give up believing in a good God and the value of a God-honoring life. Indeed, the hope-filled words of Job seem to increase as the dialogues continue. The longer his trial lasts, the more firmly Job holds to his assertion of innocence, and his assurance that there must be another explanation of his predicament. When Satan has done his worst, and can do no more to Job than take his life, Job insists on being true to his convictions. Let us turn our attention to these assertions of faith from the lips of one who might have been expected to abandon God altogether, but who held on to his integrity until the storm was past.

STUDY QUESTIONS FOR CHAPTER 3

1. This chapter mentions several Job texts still used in funeral services. Is this true of the denomination/congregation of which you are a part? If so, why, and is the use of these texts appropriate in this setting considering our understanding of their contextual meaning?

2. Discuss the suggestion that Job offers insights into the nature of suffering, and indirectly addresses the issue of ministering to suffering people.

3. The end of the chapter mentions other reactions to suffering that might have been discussed in more detail. Examine the texts referred to, and determine whether there are still other reactions to suffering not mentioned in this section.

4. "Job provides a balance for any discussion of the relationship of suffering to the character of the sufferer." In light of the analysis in this chapter, examine this statement.

4

During the Storms:
Reactions of Job—The Person of Faith

PARADOXICALLY, THE LONGER JOB suffered, the greater became his determination to persevere in hope and faith. It is this very paradox that makes the experience of Job so valuable and so instructive. In his early speeches there is more of the spirit of the perplexed questioner, the wonderer, the angry semi-doubter, revealed in his words. As the dialogues continue, Job alternates between doubting and hoping, between questioning and determining to believe whether questions are resolved or not. This wavering between attitudes continues almost to the end of Job's speeches; it can be demonstrated however, that determination increases and doubt diminishes as he comes nearer his last words. The following thoughts summarize what we might call Job's "and yet" reactions.

JOB'S SPEECHES REVEAL FLASHES OF FAITH

Job's first speech in chapter 3 is entirely negative in mood and content. Job curses his birthday, wishes he had never been born, or that he had been stillborn, or that he could find death now to release him from present misery.

> Why is light given to those in misery, and life to the bitter of soul, to those who long for death that does not come, who search for it more than for hidden treasure, who are filled with gladness and rejoice when they reach the grave? (Job 3:20–22)

Why should he not long for release? Can he be blamed for such dejection when he can say with all truthfulness, "I have no peace, no quietness; I have no rest, but only turmoil"? (Job 3:26). Here is a human being crying out for deliverance from trouble of the highest order. His words are heartbreaking, and we sympathize with Job the sufferer. Job the person of faith and hope is nowhere to be seen as yet.

Job's second speech, found in chapters 6 and 7, is also filled with complaining and crying out for answers to the question, "Why has this happened?" It is in this passage that the reactions, "I can't handle this!" "What did I do to deserve this?" "I'll never get over this!" and "Life has no meaning!" occur. Here, too, Job chastises his friends for their lack of sympathetic understanding. Just when he, a despairing man, needs their support and encouragement, they misjudge him and bring as much disappointment to him as dry stream beds bring to tired and thirsty travelers who finally arrive at an oasis only to discover it has dried up:

> But my brothers are as undependable as intermittent streams, as the streams that overflow when darkened by thawing ice and swollen with melting snow, but that cease to flow in the dry season, and in the heat vanish from their channels. Caravans turn aside from their routes; they go up to the wasteland and perish. The caravans of Tema look for water, the traveling merchants of Sheba look in hope. They are distressed because they had been confident; they arrive there only to be disappointed. Now you too have proved to be of no help; you see something dreadful and are afraid." (Job 6:15–21)

In this speech Job complains that God is singling him out, picking on him unfairly. "Why me?" he asks, and every sufferer has asked the same question, perhaps not so poetically:

> Am I the sea, or the monster of the deep, that you put me under guard? . . . What is man that you make so much of him, that you give him so much attention, that you examine him every morning and test him every moment? Will you never look away from me, or let me alone even for an instant? If I have sinned, what have I done to you, O watcher of men? Why have you made me your target? Have I become a burden to you? (Job 7:12, 17–20)

Puzzled, surprised, Job seems to believe he ought somehow to have been passed over when troubles were being handed out by the Lord. With other sufferers he seems to believe that no one has been through what he is being called upon to experience. Pain and suffering have isolated him to the extent that he feels all alone—the sole target of divine malediction:

> If only my anguish could be weighed and all my misery placed on the scales! It would outweigh the sand of the seas—no wonder my words have been impetuous [no wonder, indeed!]. The arrows of the Almighty are in me, my spirit drinks in their poison; God's terrors are marshaled against me. (Job 6:2–4)

Job knows he is speaking rashly, sometimes almost insanely, but it is the insanity of pure misery that is coming forth from his lips. And yet ...

In this same speech, filled as it is with words of perplexed discouragement, and with irrational sentiments that Job utters with an apparent sense of embarrassment, there is one ray of hope. Job is in such agony that here, as elsewhere, he wishes for the release of death. Notice, however, his protestation of innocence in the midst of this dark longing. If he should die, it would be as an innocent man, and one who, for all his groaning, had not denied his Lord:

> Oh, that I might have my request, that God would grant me what I hope for, that God would be willing to crush me, to let loose his hand and cut me off! Then I would have this consolation—my joy in unrelenting pain—that I had not denied the words of the Holy One. (Job 6:8–10)

In the prologue, Satan had stated his assurance that Job, if afflicted severely enough, would "surely curse [God] to [his] face." In this attestation in chapter 6, well along in the examination being carried out upon him, Job says perhaps more than he realizes. He has not denied God; he has not denied God's words. Neither, though he is unaware of them, has he denied the words of the Holy One that were spoken about him. Job is passing the examination at this point. Complaining and questioning are certainly part of his response; surrender to the enemy in the defeat of denying and denouncing God is not.

The third speech of Job is contained in chapters 9 and 10. The discouragement deepens; the questions about the justice of God in his dealings with his servant become more urgent, because no answers have been forthcoming. God's ways are not our ways, Job reasons. God is so great; I am so limited—what hope is there that any sense can be read into the events of my life? I suffer; there is no reason for it, only the fact that it is happening, and God, who is the author of all events, is allowing it. God must be the cause of it. "If it is not he then who is it?" (Job 9:24).

Innocent or guilty, it does not seem to matter. God has judged me. What will transpire will transpire. What's the use!

> If it is a matter of strength, he is mighty! And if it is a matter of justice, who will [who has the strength equal to his to enable one to] summon him? Even if I were innocent, my mouth would condemn me; if I were blameless, it would pronounce me guilty. (Job 9:19–20)

These words indicate Job's claustrophobic sense of being caught in forces carrying him along relentlessly. And yet . . .

Again in this speech there are shafts of brightness illuminating the gloom ever so slightly. Job will stand his ground on the issue of his innocence: "I am blameless" (9:21), he insists, and somehow he is sure God knows this fact. "Are your days like those of a mortal," he asks the Lord, "or your years like those of a man, that you must search out my faults and probe after my sin, though you know I am not guilty . . . ?" (10:5–7). The integrity is maintained, and faith in the God Who Knows is still a reality, even though this faith is seriously strained.[1]

Flashes of insight, shafts of faith shining through, and then the relapse into doubting again: this is the pattern of the speeches of Job. The flashes and the shafts are all-important, however. They serve to separate Job from those who face struggles with no faith, or with such a little faith that a small amount of suffering is able to choke it into oblivion. The speech ends on a somber note; faith seems to be far away:

> If I am guilty—woe to me! Even if I am innocent, I cannot lift my head, for I am full of shame and drowned in my affliction. If I hold my head high, you stalk me like a lion and again display your awesome power against me. You bring new witnesses against me and increase your anger toward me; your forces come against me wave upon wave. (Job 10:15–17)

---

1. Note Strahan, *Book of Job*, 12, who says, "Though indisputable facts point to an awful God who has become his Enemy, his heart assures him of a gracious God who is his Friend and has never ceased to love him. And the strangest thing in the drama is his appeal to the God of Heaven against the God of earth. The antinomy indicates that he is groping after a higher conception of God. All his wild words, in some of which he comes perilously near to anathematizing God, are directed against a pitiless and undiscriminating Force. And his new faith, which is not fabricated in the schools of logic, but forged in the furnace of affliction, is faith in a God who loves and can be loved." I agree that there is a conflict in the thinking of Job about the character of God, but would suggest that it is not a new faith being forged; rather it is the triumph of his old faith being revealed in the furnace of affliction.

Job's fourth speech is found in chapters 12 to 14. By this time, Job has come to believe that God is the author of all that happens to people, and especially is this true if one considers the misfortunes of humanity. In fact, God is pictured as involved exclusively in bringing about disaster in the world. It is he who tears down, imprisons, brings drought, devastates the land, humiliates counselors, makes fools of judges, releases wicked prisoners, dishonours priests, brings the respected to mortification, silences advisers, destroys, disperses, and deprives nations of good leadership (Job 12:14-25). All nature, Job asserts, testifies to the injustice of God's rule in the world,

> But ask the animals, and they will teach you, or the birds of the air, and they will tell you; or speak to the earth and it will teach you, or let the fish of the sea inform you. Which of all these does not know that the hand of the Lord has done this? (Job 12:7-9)

Chapter 14, we have noted, contains some of the most depressing and discouraging thoughts in the speeches of Job. "Man born of woman is of few days and full of trouble. He springs up like a flower and withers away; like a fleeting shadow, he does not endure" (Job 14:1-2). Life is full of trouble—then you die! There is more hope for a dead tree than there is for a dying human. Some life might grow out of the deadness of the tree.

> But man dies and is laid low; he breathes his last and is no more. As water disappears from the sea or a river bed becomes parched and dry, so man lies down and does not rise; till the heavens are no more, men will not awake or be roused from their sleep (Job 14:10-12). So man wastes away like something rotten, like a garment eaten by moths. (Job 13:28)

Nor is Job any less harsh with his friends in this speech. Hear his sarcasm, "Doubtless you are the people, and wisdom will die with you" (Job 12:2). "You," he says contemptuously to them, "smear me with lies; you are worthless physicians, all of you! If only you would be altogether silent! For you, that would be wisdom" (Job 13:4-5). "Your maxims are proverbs of ashes; your defenses are defenses of clay" (Job 13:12). Surely Job could not feel more alone, deserted, alienated, and friendless. And yet...

In this same despairing speech, Job utters some of the bravest words in his vocabulary as a person of faith. "I am going to keep on defending myself," he insists, "because I dare to believe God will hear me, will listen to my charges of injustice, will agree with me, and will vindicate me as his servant and righteous follower."

In this declaration of determination, Job utters what must be the most often quoted words of the book, "Though he slay me, yet will I hope in him." The sentence deserves to be set in context. He says to his counselors:

> Keep silent and let me speak... Why do I put myself in jeopardy and take my life in my hands? Though he slay me, yet will I hope in him; I will surely defend my ways to his face. Indeed, this will turn out for my deliverance, for no godless man would dare come before him! Listen carefully to my words; let your ears take in what I say. Now that I have prepared my case, I know I will be vindicated. (Job 13:13–18)

It is popularly thought that Job is saying, "Even if God takes my life, I'll continue to be a believer." In context. however, his words seem to mean, "Those who speak up to God in self defense are living dangerously. If their defense is hypocritical, they will be slain. I must speak up; I will take the chance of being put to death, because I believe so strongly in my innocence and in God's sovereign fairness. If I continue to cling to my integrity, and keep pestering heaven regarding my situation, eventually I will be heeded, and I, who have prepared my case, will be delivered and vindicated." Far from cursing God, Job is here defending God, and counting on God to defend him.

Furthermore, in the middle of the fourteenth chapter, the chapter of deep discouragement, melancholy, and near-despair, Job speaks as a believer and possessor of hope: "If a man dies," he asks, uttering a query that multitudes would echo with the utmost seriousness, "will he live again?" (Job 14:14). The Christian longs to share with a suffering Job and a questioning world the comforting and assuring words of Jesus, who said, "I am the resurrection and the life. He who believes in me will live, even though he dies; and whoever lives and believes in me will never die" (John 11:25).

Although he is unable to find comfort in the words of Jesus, Job does catch a glimpse of something hopeful for the person of faith, even though the light flashes but for a moment.

> All the days of my hard service I will wait for my renewal to come.
> You will call and I will answer you; you will long for the creature

your hands have made. Surely then you will count my steps but not keep track of my sin. My offenses will be sealed up in a bag; you will cover over my sin. (Job 14:14–17)

Job is saying, "I will wait for God. My day of release is coming. God longs for my fellowship as I long for his. A day is coming when there will be no more testing, no more concern about chastisement or punishment. I believe the day of the Lord will come for me. I will endure, waiting for release!"[2]

One can almost hear Satan groan. God's servant, tottering near the brink of absolute anguish, refuses to step over that precipice into despair. God is for me, Job protests. I know it! Against all the prevailing evidence I will believe it. My day will come!

Job's fifth speech is in chapters 16 and 17. The speech begins with more sharp words to the "friends" to whom Job is responding. It is in chapter 16 that Job gives them the name by which multitudes have come to know them, Eliphaz, Bildad, and Zophar, the "miserable comforters" of Job (Job 16:2). He asks:

Will your long-winded speeches never end? What ails you that you keep on arguing? I also could speak like you, if you were in my place; I could make fine speeches against you and shake my head at you. But my mouth would encourage you; comfort from my lips would bring you relief. (Job 16:3–5)

Encouragement, comfort, relief—these are the gifts the suffering long to receive from their visitors and would-be ministers. May all who visit the sick and suffering take seriously Job's rebukes to his comforters!

The Lord, too, is criticized again by Job, whose words indicate that he has progressed in his illness and desolation to the point of being close to death. "Surely, O God, you have worn me out . . . My spirit is broken, my days are cut short, the grave awaits me" (Job 16:7; 17:1). The examination has taken its toll. The suffering servant of God is almost finished.

---

2. Wood does not find these words nearly as hope-filled as I have interpreted them: "Even the oft-quoted question of Job: If a man die, shall he live again? (14:14) must not be used for attributing to Job a greater degree of hope than he actually possessed. These words are probably [?] a later interpolation and Job is not thinking in terms of a return from the dead." (Wood, *Job and the Human Situation*, 65). Apart from Wood's conjecture regarding interpolation, it is necessary to point out that not all translations of Job render his responses as a man of faith as positively as does the New International Version that is used throughout this book.

Not much more can be inflicted upon him before his life will come to an end. "I have sewed sackcloth over my skin and buried my brow in the dust. My face is red with weeping, deep shadows ring my eyes" (Job 16:15–16). And yet . . .

Hear the rustle of hope; see the faint light of faith, hear the words that run completely counter to the drift of this dismal conversation:

> Yet my hands have been free of violence and my prayer is pure. O earth do not cover my blood; may my cry never be laid to rest! Even now my witness is in heaven; my advocate is on high. My intercessor is my friend as my eyes pour out tears to God; on behalf of a man he pleads with God as a man pleads for his friend. (Job 16:17–21)

Remarkable words! Job says, I have a witness in heaven; I have an advocate on high; I have an intercessor who is pleading my case with God; my advocate is my friend! Of whom does Job speak? Of himself or of someone else?[3]

Is it legitimate to find a parallel in the New Testament story of the Ethiopian reading Isaiah's account of another Suffering Servant, and asking Philip the Evangelist, "'Tell me please, who is the prophet talking about, himself or someone else?' Then Philip began with that very passage of Scripture and told him the good news about Jesus" (Acts 8:34–35). Could it be that a far-off, faint and rather blurred image of the Son of God, the intercessor, the advocate of the believer who "pleads with God as a man pleads for his friend," briefly but surely passes into Job's view? However we choose to identify the object of Job's vision, it is certain that he believes that he has a friend in heaven, and that his case will be defended on his behalf by an intercessor who pleads with God for him. He is still the man of faith and integrity, no matter how many may be his words of complaint.

---

3. Again Wood, *Job and the Human Situation*, 70, is not so sure that these are hopeful words. In fact, he sees them as examples of Job's confused despair: "All that Job can do now, so long as there is breath in his sick body, is to keep on appealing. But to whom, God or man? Since neither of these is prepared to help, Job looks elsewhere. He asks that his blood will keep up a continual cry until his innocence be proved. He calls upon some witness in heaven to vouch for his good name. But such appeals are empty words that reach no ear. Yet, these supplications to imaginary helpers only illustrate Job's plight. He has reached such a state of despair that he reverts to primitive ideas about blood on the one hand, and pathetically conjures up some ill-defined heavenly witness on the other." Obviously I disagree, and prefer the interpretation that seems to come most naturally from reading the NIV.

In spite of all that has happened to him, Job is able to say, "Nevertheless [an important word in the vocabulary of the believer living in a hostile world], the righteous will hold to their ways, and those with clean hands will grow stronger" (Job 17:9).

Job's sixth speech is in chapter 19. Job's friends, who mean well and have tried so hard to justify the ways of God to Job, have become his tormenters.

> How long will you torment me and crush me with words? Ten times now you have reproached me; shamelessly you attack me. If it is true that I have gone astray, my error remains my concern alone. If indeed you would exalt yourselves above me and use my humiliation against me, then know that God has wronged me and drawn his net around me. (Job 19:2–6)

Is this a slightly oblique way of asking them to mind their own business? He does still seek their genuine friendship, however, as revealed in this plea already alluded to: "Have pity on me, my friends, have pity, for the hand of God has struck me. Why do you pursue me as God does? Will you never get enough of my flesh?" (Job 19:21–22).

Listen to the words of Job as they demonstrate how far he has gone in the direction of believing God is crushing him completely:

> He has blocked my way so I cannot pass; he has shrouded my paths in darkness. He has stripped me of my honor and removed the crown from my head. He tears me down on every side till I am gone; he uproots my hope like a tree. His anger burns against me; he counts me among his enemies. His troops advance in force; they build a siege ramp against me and encamp around my tent. (Job 19:8–12)

It sounds as though Job is about to give up entirely and die forlorn and faithless. And yet . . .

This chapter, containing as it does angry words against friends and accusations against God, also contains one of the most beautiful songs of hope and comfort to appear in the whole of the Scriptures. In the midst of the darkness, with death so painfully near, and all of the meaningless mystery of what has happened remaining, Job proclaims the words that form the heart of Handel's Messiah. He says, "Oh, that my words were recorded, that they were written on a scroll, that they were inscribed with an iron tool on lead, or engraved in rock forever" (Job 19:23–24). Job, your prayer has been answered. Your words have been preserved for posterity—as part of the sacred Scriptures generations have read them and been blessed by your songs in the night:

> I know that my Redeemer lives, and that in the end he will stand upon the earth. And after my skin has been destroyed, yet in my flesh I will see God; I myself will see him with my own eyes—I, and not another. How my heart yearns within me! (Job 19:25–27)[4]

We want to read into this song all of our New Testament understandings of Jesus our blessed Redeemer. Indeed he will stand upon the earth as our reconciler and future King. We know, too, that we will see the Lord after our resurrection. Our hearts, too, yearn within us as we long for his second coming and the end of this age of waiting and groaning. With Paul we can say, especially in times of stress and sorrow and physical suffering, that we long to "depart and be with Christ, which is better by far" (Phil 1:23), and "we prefer to be away from the body and at home with the Lord" (2 Cor 5:8).[5]

---

4. Strahan, *Book of Job*, 13, says, "It is one of the presuppositions of the drama that this world is the only field in which divine justice is exercised, and there is at first no suggestion that the wrongs of the present may be righted in an after-life. But when it becomes apparent to Job that he can never get justice in this world, his mind leaps instinctively to the thought of a posthumous vindication. From the depths of despair he suddenly rises to grapple with the last enemy, to put his foot on the neck of Death. For at least one supreme moment he stands convinced that as a disembodied spirit he will be recalled from Sheol to hear himself justified and to see his Vindicator."

5. Wood, *Job and the Human Situation*, 76, again argues with any attempt to put Job's words into a faith-filled light. Commenting on 19:25, he says, "Unfortunately, these words cannot be accepted simply as they stand. The Hebrew text and versions in other languages are very unsatisfactory. Verses 25–27 are only translatable on the basis of a considerable amount of conjecture. In the hope of clarifying our explanation of the passage, we suggest the following tentative translation of these verses: 25. For I know that my redeemer lives, and at last he will stand on the earth; 26. and after my skin has been thus destroyed, then without my flesh I shall see God, 27. Whom I shall see on my side, and my eyes shall behold, and not another. My heart faints within me!" It is strange that Wood desires to be so careful about ascribing hopeful attitudes to Job, at the same time as he presents us with a translation of these verses which in no way takes away from our assertion that they are the words of a believer, with all the limitations of Old Testament faith, of course. All scholars agree with the explanation of the difficulty of the Hebrew in this, as in many Job passages. Many note, for example, that it seems unclear whether Job states that he will see God in his body, or apart from his body. That Job is sure he will see God, for himself, is rarely contested. Note Archer's discussion of this passage in *Survey of Old Testament Introduction*, 465, where he says, "It is fair to conclude that a Hebrew listener would have understood the statement to mean, 'And from the vantage point of my flesh I shall see God.'"

Are all of these allusions to be read into Job's beautiful and brave words?[6] Probably not, if we intend to suggest that Job even for a moment understood all of this glorious New Testament truth. We would be very unkind to Job, however, if we tried to suggest that the song of chapter 19 is lacking in at least a good measure of bright hopefulness. Faith again breaks through the barriers caused by circumstances, ignorance, and even very human doubt. "I know! He lives! He will stand! I will see God! I will see him! With my own eyes!" This is the voice of faith, and the voice of faith is the voice of triumph. Curse God and die? Curse God to his face? No! Never! "I shall see God!" And faith in the hour of greatest darkness was rewarded, not at the resurrection, but at the end of the examination, after the storm had passed. In Job 42:5 Job was able to say, "My ears had heard of you but now my eyes have seen you."[7]

---

6. Wood, *Job and the Human Situation*, 154–58, adds an appendix in which he treats this passage at some length. Although he wishes to be extremely careful not to read more into this nineteenth chapter than is warranted, his conclusions are not unlike mine: "There is real wisdom in claiming less rather than more for this passage. We must take care we are not led too far away from the human situation Job was set in, by our Christian presuppositions. Yet, we hasten to add, we must not go to the other extreme and deny the truth of our Christian presuppositions. Our Christian faith is an exceedingly important element in the human situation . . . Job's appeal to his unknown, undefined and even vaguely conceived Redeemer is, in the light of Christian faith, to be regarded as a foreshadowing of a truth that was to become clearer with the entry of Jesus Christ into the human situation. In his situation, Job was groping after a Redeemer who would act on his behalf. The figure eluded him . . . But from the perspective granted to Christian faith . . . we can believe what Job was not able to say: there is a Redeemer, the Divine Redeemer, known to us as the Savior of all men, including Job and ourselves, and He is Jesus Christ, God and man" (p. 158). Waltke, *Old Testament Theology*, 936, states, "After this confession [19:25–27], Job does not doubt again. Job is 'patient/persevering' (James 5:11 contra Job 21:4), not in serenity nor in tranquility, but in the energy to persist in faith . . . in the midst of contrary experiences. In other words . . . in spite of life's absurdities, his faith wins out."

7. Strahan, *Book of Job*, 176, says, "The word 'Vindicator' is the nearest equivalent to the Hebrew *Goel*, though 'Redeemer' may quite well be used, provided it is defined as man's Deliverer, not from sin, but from unmerited wrong—the Redeemer of one's honor. In the language of men, the *Goel* was the nearest blood-relation, on whom civil law imposed the duty of redeeming the property or person of his kinsman, and criminal law that of avenging his kinsman's blood if it was unjustly shed." Strahan nicely describes the increasingly positive nature of Job's faith: "If there is a logical progress, a gradual evolution of ideas, in the drama, what Job expects is not only a posthumous vindication, but his own recall to hear it and to see his Vindicator. In 14:14 ff he seems emphatically to deny the possibility of a life after death, yet he is evidently fascinated by the idea. In 16:18ff he expresses his faith in a Witness and Voucher who, after his death, will maintain his right. And now he expresses the conviction that not only the claims of

Job's seventh speech is in chapter 21. This chapter reveals Job as a man almost totally convinced that popular understandings of justice are entirely false. People assume that God blesses the righteous and punishes the wicked. Precisely the opposite is the case, Job states. The whole scheme of a world where whatever one sows is reaped in this life seldom comes to pass. Wicked people live a long time, their families are blessed and no calamity or wrath ever comes upon them.

> Yet how often is the lamp of the wicked snuffed out? How often does calamity come upon them, the fate God allows in his anger? How often are they like straw before the wind, like chaff swept away by a gale? It is said, "God stores up a man's punishment for his sons." Let him repay the man himself, so that he will know it! Let his own eyes see his destruction; let him drink of the wrath of the Almighty. For what does he care about the family he leaves behind when his allotted months come to an end? (Job 21:17-21)

Here is the voice of Job the suffering human, who surmises, from the fact that he as a good man has suffered, that the law of retribution must be: the good suffer, the evil prosper. Satan would be glad to hear these words from Job; after all, the logical conclusion to be drawn from this reasoning would be: turn to evil, and suffering will diminish. Godless people are blessed. There is great gain in godlessness.

This is not the conclusion of Job, the man of faith, however. His conclusion does not align itself with his train of thought, but no matter. Almost incidentally as he laments the prosperity of the wicked, he affirms, "so I stand aloof from the counsel of the wicked" (Job 21:16). Job is inconsistent, to be sure, but this is a blessed inconsistency. He insists on remaining a man who shuns evil, even when reason and experience would call for surrender to that very evil. If Satan is delighted at Job's misconceived questions regarding the justice of God, his delight is short-lived. We can only surmise that Job realizes that his thoughts regarding the prosperity of wicked people are incorrect, based as they are upon his present agony. Who triumphs in this sad chapter, the Job of doubt or the

---

ideal justice, but the human heart's deepest longing will be satisfied by the summoning of the injured dead back to life to be present at his own vindication. Further than this Job does not go ... After his death he shall awake again to full consciousness, and shall see God—with whom be the rest!" (p. 177).

Job of faith? This simple statement of determination to avoid the counsel of the ungodly provides the answer.

Job's eighth speech is in chapters 23 and 24. In this speech, Job asks, "Oh, God, where are you?" Job longs for God, cries out for him, and indicates that he would go anywhere if only he could be assured that God would be there at the end of the journey. For all his longing, God is not to be found. Around Job there is nothing but darkness. And yet ...

"Yet I am not silenced by the darkness, by the thick darkness that covers my face" (Job 23:17). If God could be found, if only he would appear, Job is sure that the outcome would be favorable for him:

> If only I knew where to find him; if only I could go to his dwelling! I would state my case before him and fill my mouth with arguments. I would find out what he would answer me and consider what he would say. Would he oppose me with great power? No, he would not press charges against me. There an upright man could present his case before him, and I would be delivered forever from my judge. (Job 23:3–7)

Job will not be overcome by the prevailing darkness. He will hang on to his integrity, believing that once God appears justice will prevail, for God is righteous and his presence is a place of safety.

In chapter 24, Job relapses into a complaint regarding the inequities of life. The theme again is in opposition to the constantly stated thesis of his friends. They say, over and over, that the righteous are always rewarded and the wicked are always punished in this life. From his perspective on the other side of blessing, Job sees things as precisely opposite. The wicked are blessed, the good people of the earth—the poor, the needy, the widow—suffer interminably. And yet ...

Before he engages in this tirade regarding cosmic injustice, Job speaks as one who still believes God is just, and his ways are fair. His speech is so positive and expresses his faith so beautifully, the reader is convinced that this is the real Job speaking, the Job who is in his right mind revealing the content of his deepest convictions:

> But he knows the way I take; when he has tested me, I will come forth as gold. My feet have closely followed his steps; I have kept his way without turning aside. I have not departed from the commands of his lips; I have treasured the words of his mouth more than my daily bread. (Job 23:10–12)

During the Storms: Reactions of Job—The Person of Faith

Again in this passage, Job asserts his belief in the God Who Knows; the God whose way is worth following, whose commands are worth obeying, whose words are precious and to be savored. Here, too, is the determination to steadfastly endure the testing, with the assurance that the Job who endures will be a better Job, tried as precious metal in the fire of affliction. This is the speech of a man who is already pure gold, and the purity remains!⁸

Job's ninth speech, his last words in his dialogue with his friends, is in chapters 26 to 31. With Bildad's short and miserable parting shot in chapter 25, the words of the three friends come to an end. They have had their say and God will rebuke them for many of their unkind, insensitive, and irrelevant words.

What will Job say at the last? Will he finally give up his faith, and curse God, and die? For death seems not far away: "And now my life ebbs away; days of suffering grip me. Night pierces my bones; my gnawing pains never rest . . . [God] throws me into the mud, and I am reduced to dust and ashes" (Job 30:16–19). There is still the voice of distressful complaint to be sure,

> I cry out to you, O God, but you do not answer; I stand up, but you merely look at me. You turn on me ruthlessly; with the might of your hand you attack me. You snatch me up and drive me before the wind; you toss me about in the storm." (Job 30:20–22)

Chapter 30 is filled with a bitter lament concerning his present desolation. The previous chapter had described his quiet, prosperous God-filled life before the storm. Chapter 30 begins, "But now . . ." What a contrast is here revealed! When things were going well he had reasoned,

---

8. Strahan, *Book of Job*, 208–9, is right when he says, "Job is not speaking of the refining effect of suffering, and there is no evidence that such a thought (which is elaborated by Elihu) ever occurred to him. What the Heb. word for 'try' suggests is the testing, first of metals, and then of characters . . . Job is placed in circumstances in which it is impossible to have any false humility; he knows his own moral worth, and asserts that, when the Assayer tries him, He will find not dross, but gold. The whole verse is one of Job's most characteristic utterances, expressing his ineradicable sense of God's righteousness (which has so often been questioned by himself), as well as of his own (which has been so often questioned by others)." There seems to be no reason to follow Strahan's argument that closes this discussion, however. Precisely the opposite of Strahan's conclusion is more probably the case. Here Strahan says, "His good conscience is the foundation of his faith in the goodness of the universe. Sure of himself, he is again becoming 'very sure of God.'"

> I thought, "I will die in my own house, my days as numerous as the grains of sand. My roots will reach to the water, and the dew will lie all night on my branches. My glory will remain fresh in me, the bow ever new in my hand." (Job 29:18–20)

In the midst of the storm the glory has departed, however. "Terrors overwhelm me; my dignity is driven away as by the wind, my safety vanishes like a cloud" (Job 30:15). All who once respected Job and who were the objects of his kindness and generosity, now mock him, detest him, avoid him, even dare to spit in his face (Job 30:1, 9–11). And God? Why, it is he who "has unstrung my bow and afflicted me" (Job 30:11). And yet . . .

In this last speech, Job does express his belief that the wicked are not the objects of divine blessing after all. Job knows, as well as his friends, the truth that justice will eventually, ultimately, prevail.

> For what hope has the godless when he is cut off, when God takes away his life? Does God listen to his cry when distress comes upon him? Will he find delight in the Almighty? Will he call upon God at all times? . . . Here is the fate God allots to the wicked, the heritage a ruthless man receives from the Almighty: However many his children, their fate is the sword; his offspring will never have enough to eat." (Job 27:8–14)

Job has been describing a world turned upside down with righteousness on the scaffold and injustice on the throne. Of course he has overreacted to his trouble and to the all-too-pat explanations of his friends. In this passage, he indicates that for all the qualifications that need to be placed upon the idea that all judgment against evil is not meted out in this life, the fact of the matter is that God sees and knows and will judge aright.[9]

---

9. Commentators find it difficult to understand Job's denunciation of the wicked here. Many try to reorganize the passage so that it belongs to the speech of Eliphaz or Bildad. But Archer, *Survey of Old Testament Introduction,* 463, is probably right when he says that this is not at all necessary. The words are Job's own: "Adherents to the multiple-source theory often single out chapter 27 as an interpolation, because it contains a denunciation of the wicked far more in harmony with what the three comforters have been saying in the earlier chapters than with the defensive position Job has maintained . . . On the other hand it should be recognized that Job himself at no point offers any defense for the sinner or holds out any hope for him that he would escape God's judgment in the final outcome. Actually what he does in chapter 27 is skillfully to turn the tables on his unjust accusers who have dogmatically insisted that his calamity must be a consequence of hidden and unconfessed sin. Then, insisting on his own unqualified

We spent much time earlier examining chapters 29 and 31 in some detail, in an effort to understand the kind of person Job was, as he describes his character to us in these chapters. We discovered someone to be greatly admired, someone who enjoyed the pleasure of the company of God, and who used his godly understanding and material wealth to bless the lives of everyone with whom he came into contact. Job, the servant of God and the servant of righteousness—here is the man whom God praises and whom Satan so furiously attacks.

Have these attacks changed the man? His physical appearance has changed; so has his station in life; so has his peace of mind. Relationships have changed drastically. Close friends have become suspicious enemies. His family has been decimated and devastated. Is there anything about Job that has not changed? How in the world could there be anything changeless left?

Hear Job's climactic declaration in Job 27:2–6, a speech that combines something of the human believer and the believing human, but which is dominated by the believer, the person of faith:

> As surely as God lives, who has denied me justice, the Almighty, who has made me taste bitterness of soul, as long as I have life within me, the breath of God in my nostrils, my lips will not speak wickedness, and my tongue will utter no deceit. I will never admit you are in the right; till I die I will not deny my integrity. I will maintain my righteousness and never let go of it; my conscience will not reproach me as long as I live. (Job 27:2–6)

God the Almighty lives; his breath is within me; I will not deny the Lord! Neither will I give up on my determination to be the best person I can be even though I suffer and do not know why. Take my life; you cannot take my character! This you cannot change! These are Job's last words, and they are defiant words: No matter what else happens, here I stand!

Here is the climax of the book of Job. Job has been tossed by the storm almost into oblivion. He will not give in, however. No matter what else happens he will maintain faith and integrity. He will be forever God's servant, pleasing to God as a person of piety and purity.

---

adherence to the cause of righteousness, decency, and justice, Job very logically passes on to express his expectation that his slanderous accusers will themselves taste the fruit of their injustice in blackening his character."

Satan can do no more. He has brought every force imaginable against Job. He has attacked Job's family, his possessions, his reputation, his body, his sanity, his dignity. Job has reeled under the many barrages hurled against him. Many times his words have been upsetting, unorthodox, shocking. He has spoken as a deeply grieving human, as a disease-ridden patient, as a confused and pain-maddened sufferer. He has never spoken as an unbelieving sinner, however. Satan was so sure Job would fall. Here, at the end of the ordeal, Job, stooped over by sickness, stands spiritually tall and erect as God's creature, God's child, and God's servant. Satan can leave the field now. He has been defeated on his own turf. Faith and hope have driven him from the battle. God and his servant have won the day.

THE ODE TO WISDOM: JOB'S PHILOSOPHY OF WHAT REALLY MATTERS

The chapters containing Job's last words include the beautiful Ode to Wisdom in chapter 28. If Job spoke these words, they are certainly the most positive he uttered in all his speeches. Perhaps they are a continuation of his thoughts about the greatness of God that comprise the major portion of chapter 26, especially verses 7 to 14.

> He spreads out the northern skies over empty space; he suspends the earth over nothing. He wraps up the waters in his clouds, yet the clouds do not burst under their weight. He covers the face of the full moon, spreading the clouds over it . . . By his power he churned up the sea . . . by his breath the skies became fair . . . and these are but the outer fringe of his works; how faint the whisper we hear of him!

Here is a Job we have heard from only faintly up until this speech. He seems to be seeing things so differently, so much more positively for longer periods than in previous speeches.

Chapter 27 contains the words that we have described as the climax of the book, Job's declaration of determination (Job 27:3–6), and it concludes with his assertion of the certainty of the destruction that will ultimately come upon the wicked. Here is another indication that the bitter questions about the justice of God are being laid to rest in Job's thinking. Then comes chapter 28, the song that tells where true wisdom is to be found. All of this is evidence that Job's last words are his most victorious words, even though he has no idea that the storm, which has been raging around him, is about to come to an end.

Chapter 28 is unique in Job. It sounds like it ought to be a key chapter in the book of Proverbs, dealing as it does with the source and nature of true wisdom. There is nothing in it of suffering, questioning, agonizing, and seeking answers to the hard questions of human existence. It is rather a cool reflection upon humanity as a discoverer of things that are valuable and precious. To say this is, of course, to suggest that the chapter is indeed related to the search of the book of Job for valuable and precious insights into the meaning of suffering for the child of God.[10]

The first eleven verses of chapter 28 describe humans as tremendously resourceful and versatile in their ability to outsmart nature in unearthing her many hidden treasures, the precious metals and stones that lie hidden beneath the surface of the earth. But humanity, ever so wise and ingenious in discovering and appropriating these tangible treasures, is described in verses 12 to 22 as hopelessly unable to find the greatest treasures of all—wisdom and understanding.

These words about humanity's intellectual capacity to discover and develop natural resources, and conversely about the seeming inability of people, however mentally gifted, to find answers to some of the most fundamental moral, ethical, and social questions concerning human existence and survival, have tremendous contemporary significance. A modern paraphrase of the gist of this chapter might sound like this: "Scientific and technological knowledge is incredible in its breadth and importance. The way of science is valuable and indispensable in gaining

---

10. Many commentators agree with Strahan that this speech is not to be considered part of the poetic dialogue: "This fine poem . . . can scarcely have formed a part of the original drama," Strahan says in *Book of Job*, 232. Believing as I do in the unity of Job, I do not feel obliged to agree. Archer defends the belief that the chapter belongs to the poem, and that the sentiments expressed in it are Job's, (*Survey of Old Testament Introduction*, 463). Harrison's words (*Introduction to the Old Testament*, 1034) are apropos: "Many of the suggested textual reconstructions have been extremely subjective, and the omissions appear to have been prompted by little more than arbitrary judgments. Typical were the opinions of many authors in considering that the superb hymn on divine wisdom in chapter 28 was an editorial addition that had formed no part of the original principal work, although according to some it could have been an independent composition of the author. While the poem unquestionably interrupts the soliloquy of Job . . . there seem to be valid exegetical reasons for assuming its logical connections with the surrounding passages . . . It seems at least probable, therefore, that the author of the Hymn of Wisdom is also the composer of the divine discourses, and by implication of the work as a whole."

certain kinds of understanding. There is another kind of knowledge that people need in order to function and thrive, however. The only source of this knowledge—true wisdom to understand life, to see it as a whole, and to live it well and successfully—is found in God."

The whole passage stating the value and source of wisdom deserves quotation:

> Where does wisdom come from? Where does understanding dwell? . . . God understands the way to it and he alone knows where it dwells, for he views the ends of the earth and sees everything under the heavens. When he established the force of the wind and measured out the waters, when he made a decree for the rain and a path for the thunderstorm, then he looked at wisdom and appraised it; he confirmed and tested it. And he said to man, "The fear of the Lord—that is wisdom, and to shun evil is understanding." (Job 28:20–28)

This conclusion sounds so much like Proverbs that it is easy to understand why many commentators believe the book of Job belongs to the genre of Wisdom literature, as does Proverbs. The book, say these thinkers, comes from the wisdom age—perhaps the age of Solomon, or, some say, perhaps even later. Whatever the date, the truth of the verse stands. Wisdom, as the Scriptures understand it, is more than intellectual; it has a spiritual (the fear of the Lord) and a moral/ethical (depart from evil) dimension as well.

In the Old Testament, the wise person is not only the clever person; to be wise one must be godly as well, perhaps we might say predominantly so. To be wise one must also be good. One who shuns evil is one who possesses understanding. Godless, evil people, however well educated, however able to understand the wisdom of this world, are considered by the Bible (as described especially by Proverbs) as fools. The wise person is the godly person; the wise person is the righteous person. The source of this wisdom is God himself.

If this poem in honor of wisdom was uttered by Job, and if this section is part of his final attestation of innocence, it confirms God's affirmation to Satan: "Job is a godly man; he is a good man." In chapters 29 to 31 Job will explain what it meant for him to be God's servant, and what it meant for him to shun evil and pursue genuine goodness. Anticipating all of this self-disclosure, Job intimates in chapter 28, "My determination is to remain godly and good—I will be truly wise!" Regardless of the circumstances through which one passes, the wise way is the way of trust in God, seeking always to do what is right.

A CATALOGUE OF JOB'S POSITIVE FAITH-AFFIRMING STATEMENTS

Oh, that I might have my request, that God would grant me what I hope for, that God would be willing to crush me, to let loose his hand and cut me off! Then I would have this consolation—my joy in unrelenting pain—that I had not denied the words of the Holy One. (Job 6:8–10)

"I am blameless" (Job 9:21), he insists, and somehow he is sure that God knows this fact. "Are your days like those of a mortal," he asks the Lord, "or your years like those of a man, that you must search out my faults and probe after my sin—though you know I am not guilty?" (Job 10:5–7)

Keep silent and let me speak . . . Why do I put myself in jeopardy and take my life in my hands? Though he slay me, yet will I hope in him; I will surely defend my ways to his face. Indeed, this will turn out for my deliverance, for no godless man would dare come before him! Listen carefully to my words; let your ears take in what I say. Now that I have prepared my case, I know I will be vindicated. (Job 13:13–18)

All the days of my hard service I will wait for my renewal to come. You will call and I will answer you; you will long for the creature your hands have made. Surely then you will count my steps but not keep track of my sin. My offenses will be sealed up in a bag; you will cover over my sin Yet my hands have been free of violence and my prayer is pure. (Job 14:14–17)

O earth do not cover my blood; may my cry never be laid to rest! Even now my witness is in heaven; my advocate is on high. My intercessor is my friend as my eyes pour out tears to God; on behalf of a man he pleads with God as a man pleads for his friend. (Job 16:17–21)

I know that my Redeemer lives, and that in the end he will stand upon the earth. And after my skin has been destroyed, yet in my flesh I will see God; I myself will see him with my own eyes—I, and not another. How my heart yearns within me! (Job 19:25–27)

> If only I knew where to find him; if only I could go to his dwelling! I would state my case before him and fill my mouth with arguments. I would find out what he would answer me and consider what he would say. Would he oppose me with great power? No, he would not press charges against me. There an upright man could present his case before him, and I would be delivered forever from my judge. (Job 23:3–7)

> But he knows the way I take; when he has tested me, I will come forth as gold. My feet have closely followed his steps; I have kept his way without turning aside. I have not departed from the commands of his lips; I have treasured the words of his mouth more than my daily bread. (Job 23:10–12)

> As surely as God lives, who has denied me justice, the Almighty, who has made me taste bitterness of soul, as long as I have life within me, the breath of God in my nostrils, my lips will not speak wickedness, and my tongue will utter no deceit. I will never admit you are in the right; till I die I will not deny my integrity. I will maintain my righteousness and never let go of it; my conscience will not reproach me as long as I live. (Job 27:2–6)

STUDY QUESTIONS FOR CHAPTER 4

1. In what ways does Job's faith assist or retard his ability to cope with the tragedies that come upon him?

2. Define faith as it applies to the experience of Job. Compare Job's faith with the faith described in Hebrews chapter 11.

3. Have you found it to be generally true of others as of Job that "determination increases and doubt diminishes as he came nearer his last words?"

4. In your experience do people suffering unbearably often speak words that border on what might be termed temporary insanity? How do we respond in these situations?

5. How should/do we respond to suffering people who have become convinced that God is behind their suffering and the cause of it?

6. What do you say when suffering people assert that God is to be blamed for all the world's ills?

7. Job is sometimes pretty hard on his friends. How do you as counselor take/handle criticism?

8. "Encouragement, comfort, relief these are the gifts the suffering long to receive . . ." How can we be sure we are delivering these consistently? Are there times for rebukes and chastisements in ministry to people in situations like Job's?

9. How do you respond to the severe physical deterioration of intensely suffering people?

10. What is Job asking for when he says, Pity me my friends?"

11. "I know that my redeemer lives . . ." Discuss this passage in the light of the several suggested interpretations. Is it a powerful faith statement or does its optimism need qualification?

12. The Ode to Wisdom: spoken by Job? Why is it here? Discuss Wisdom Literature and Job's place within it.

5

During the Storms: The Reactions of the Miserable Comforters

How do people respond and react to trouble when it comes? We have considered the reactions of Job, the believer who is so very human, and the reactions of Job the human being who is, to the end, a believer. What of the reactions and responses of Job's three friends, Eliphaz the Temanite, Bildad the Shuhite, and Zophar the Naamathite? It is one thing to consider the reactions of the sufferer to his plight; what about the reactions of those looking on? What can we learn from these men who were supposed to be friends and comforters?

Job's three friends really have very little to say to him. Their speeches are interspersed with those of Job in the poetical section of the book, and they take up several chapters of dialogue. Still, the substance of what they have to say can be briefly summarized. Job, they come to believe, is guilty of some misdeed, some hidden sin. God is justly punishing him. That is the answer to the problem of his suffering. Suffering always indicates the presence of wickedness. God judges sin and visits the sinner with suffering. Righteous people are always blessed; sinners are always visited with suffering. Job is suffering. Therefore, he must be God's enemy. There must be something in the life of Job that is punishable, and condemnable.[1]

---

1. Note Strahan's neat summary of the friends' theology: "Eliphaz the seer, Bildad the traditionalist, Zophar the ordinary zealot, have all of them great thoughts of the absolute power, the perfect wisdom, the ideal justice of God. They contend that they are striving to keep the nation's sacred heritage pure and intact. What they do not see is that the new conditions in which they live imperatively demand a modification of the nation's faith. Their fundamental error is that they refuse to admit patent facts, and it is the fruitful cause of others. Constituting themselves special pleaders on behalf of God, they become so enmeshed in scholastic jargon that they cease to be conscious of the poignant realities with which they trifle. They sacrifice their friend to their creed" (*Book of Job*, 10).

If Job would only be honest, they reason, if he would come out into the open with God and repent, the suffering could end and the good days could return. Defending himself as he does, protesting his innocence continually, only prolongs Job's agony. If he is blind to his own guilt, his friends will do their best to open his eyes to its reality. This is their mission, and they intend to be true to it. When it becomes clear to them that Job is not listening, not heeding their exhortation to come clean with God, they heap scorn and bitter verbal animosity upon him. After all, the ways of God must be defended, and who better than they to do the defending? If they must describe God's activity in the life of this sufferer, they must also pronounce God's judgment upon this callous, self-righteous, blasphemous sinner. Such is their assessment of Job and his predicament.

HELPFUL REACTIONS AT FIRST

Job's friends start out well in their mission of comfort. The Prologue describes them as coming from some distance, planning their rendezvous, putting themselves out to visit their grieving friend. When they arrive on the scene of Job's disasters, they are appalled at his physical appearance. How his troubles have changed and disfigured him!

> When Job's three friends ... heard about all the troubles that had come upon him, they set out from their homes and met together by agreement to go and sympathize with him and comfort him. When they saw him from a distance, they could hardly recognize him; they began to weep aloud, and they tore their robes and sprinkled dust on their heads. Then they sat on the ground with him for seven days and seven nights. No one said a word to him, because they saw how great his suffering was. (Job 2:11–13)

They do not desert Job, even though he is obviously not a pleasant companion, to say the least. Instead of beginning immediately to minister to him with speeches of comfort or exhortation, they sit down with him, and mourn with him silently for a whole week. How admirable is their silence, and their patient waiting and weeping with Job!

It is Job who breaks the silence in the third chapter, and his words are filled with half-mad ravings about wishing for his life to end. How will they respond? Will they take Job literally as he speaks of a longing for death? Or will they understand that he is speaking as a man in deep anguish? Will they continue their silent vigil, and if they speak will it be words of consolation and quiet understanding and companionship that they utter? Let us summarize the reactions of each friend in turn. Perhaps we will see in these reactions insights into how one ought to behave and what one ought to say when in the presence of a person who seeks human comradeship in a day of great trouble.

The Reactions of Eliphaz the Temanite

Eliphaz is the first to answer Job's complaints. He begins his speech softly, with words of praise for Job as a man who had in better times ministered to other sufferers with his words of strength and cheer. Noticeably absent, however, is any word of sympathy, any gesture of understanding. Instead, this first speech in chapters 4 and 5 is marked by a tone of detached impersonality.[2]

Having reminded Job that as a pillar of his community, Job had offered kind words to sufferers in days gone by, Eliphaz proceeds to offer the "helpful" revelation, "Now it's your turn, Job! Give yourself some of your own medicine. Physician, heal yourself!" This kind of taunt was cruelly tossed at Jesus on the cross (Matt 27:39–43 par). Although slightly more polished in presentation, it does seem to be part of Eliphaz's initial counsel to Job.

> Your words have supported those who stumbled; you have strengthened faltering knees. But now trouble comes to you, and you are discouraged; it strikes you and you are dismayed. Should not your piety be your confidence and your blameless ways your hope?" (Job 4:4–6)

There is a hint here that Eliphaz believes this suffering to be something that will pass away soon. He is not yet convinced that Job is a vile sinner deserving a long period of agony.

---

2. Of Eliphaz's first speech, Strahan says, "The discourse is a remarkable performance, brilliant throughout in its phrasing, and rising artistically to a noble climax. It presents not a few great and impressive ideas clothed in exquisite diction. But it has several serious blemishes. It does not contain a single word of genuine sympathy. Though addressed to a friend in the extremity of tragic sorrow, it betrays no sense of the sadness of things. It breaks the seven days' silence with the words, not of a comforter but of a moralist, not of a tender-hearted friend but of a theologian chilled by his creed" (*Book of Job*, 59). Rohr, *Job and the Mystery of Suffering*, 48–49, presents an interesting contrast between the speeches of Job and his friends. He suggests that Job is one of the greatest books on prayer ever written. The friends speak about God. Job is the only one who speaks to God, some 58 times!

Eliphaz seems to believe that what has happened to Job has come upon him for some slight misdemeanor. Job needs a brief period of punishment to bring him back into line with God's purposes. If Job will only yield now, humble himself and grovel in repentance, all will be well:

"Blessed is the man whom God corrects; so do not despise the discipline of the Almighty. For he wounds, but he also binds up, he injures but his hands also heal" (Job 5:17–18). "If it were I, I would appeal to God; I would lay my cause before him"(Job 5:8). "[Then] From six calamities he will rescue you; in seven no harm will befall you" (Job 5:19).

The problem with this advice is not that it is bad counsel as it stands, or that it is necessarily theologically inaccurate. What is wrong with this admonishment is that it is a prescription based upon a completely incorrect diagnosis. Job, we know, is not being corrected or disciplined by God. God praises Job, and has his own very important reasons for allowing his servant to be subjected to severe testing. Eliphaz urges Job to appeal to God. Job does that repeatedly, and it seems that his appeals are prayers offered to skies of brass. How cruel to reinforce Job's own growing conviction that it is God who is wounding him, God who is injuring him.

Eliphaz believes his theological analysis is correct. It is his duty as a spokesperson for God to explain God's directives and to bring Job into line with them. The only problem is that Eliphaz is wrong, and entirely off center in his assessment of this particular situation.

This reaction of Eliphaz to Job's suffering serves as a warning to us as we are called upon to minister to those who are in trouble of one kind or another. All too often when a suffering person asks the inevitable question, "Why is this happening?" we feel we must immediately come up with just the right answer. Second guessing the Lord is a very dangerous occupation, however.

I admire Eliphaz for coming to be with Job. I see it as a kind and noble gesture that this man gave up time to be with his friend when that friend was in great need. Eliphaz was right in taking Job's situation seriously, but he was wrong in taking himself as a theological counselor too seriously. He did not know the facts. He assumed too much. His understanding of God and his dealings with his creatures was far too limited. He might have admitted that, and still been a great help and support to Job. Failing to make such an admission, and insisting on the correctness of his diagnosis, Eliphaz became part of the very problem he came to help alleviate.

In this first speech, Eliphaz shares with Job an amazing nocturnal vision that has been supernaturally granted to him. In excited tones he explains the meaning of his frightening dream:

> Fear and trembling seized me and made all my bones shake. A spirit glided past my face, and the hair on my body stood on end. It stopped, but I could not tell what it was. A form stood before my eyes, and I heard a hushed voice: "Can a mortal be more righteous than God? Can a man be more pure than his Maker? If God places no trust in his servants, if he charges his angels with error, how much more those who live in houses of clay, whose foundations are in the dust, who are crushed more readily than a moth!" (Job 4:14–19)

Most significant in the light of what we have said at length about Job and his trial is Eliphaz's phrase, "God places no trust in his servants." If God never trusts an angel, how much less would he ever trust a lowly human! Eliphaz and his two fellow counselors often repeat this idea regarding the impossibility of believing that God could be pleased with any human being. Their insistence upon this theological belief increases as Job protests his innocence of any sin worthy of the degree of suffering he is passing through.

When we review the second speech of Eliphaz in chapter 15, we realize how much he has become convinced that Job is guilty of serious sin. Having listened to the intervening dialogues, Eliphaz has become very angry with Job. His anger is so apparent in his words, the reader can almost feel the heat of his wrath:

> Would a wise man answer with empty notions or fill his belly with the hot east wind? Would he argue with useless words, with speeches that have no value? But you even undermine piety and hinder devotion to God. Your sin prompts your mouth; you adopt the tongue of the crafty. Your own mouth condemns you, not mine; your own lips testify against you. (Job 15:2–6)

Has Job dared to state that he is innocent? Has he said that he is pure and upright? These words are enough to condemn any sinner. As he has stated in his first speech, Eliphaz is sure that no man could ever be considered upright in the eyes of the Lord.

During the Storms: The Reactions of the Miserable Comforters 97

> What is man, that he could be pure, or one born of woman, that he could be righteous? If God places no trust in his holy ones, if even the heavens are not pure in his eyes, how much less man, who is vile and corrupt, who drinks up evil like water. (Job 15:14–16)

These words speak for themselves as far as their comforting and encouraging value to Job are concerned. Their undue pessimism with regard to human nature is also disturbing. Here is a view that teaches that even redeemed humans are incapable of pleasing their heavenly Father. Holding such a view produces cynicism and suspicion even with regard to a friend of long standing whose reputation as a man of God and friend of humanity has been above reproach.

Here is the doctrine of human depravity carried to undue lengths, untempered by a view of God's ability to so develop the character of his child that God could speak highly of a man's loyalty to himself. Eliphaz is unable to believe that a servant of God could ever, through faith and obedience, merit the trust of the Almighty. Surely the story of Job has much to teach all who hold similar ideas even today.

All three of Job's counselors try very hard to be impersonal in their windy speeches. They resist the temptation to become explicit with Job—to accuse him of specific sins that they are aware of in his life and for which they believe he is being tormented. They describe evil men in the third person, as though they are speaking of some abstract sinner, but there is usually something barbed in their words that gives them away. They are indeed talking about Job, and their very indirectness, smacking of hypocritical cowardice, frustrates the reader, even as it must have infuriated Job.

This indirectness is illustrated in verses 20–35 of chapter 15. A few quotations will serve as examples.

> All his days the wicked man [read Job] suffers torment, the ruthless through all the years stored up for him. Terrifying sounds fill his ears; when all seems well, marauders attack him. He despairs of escaping the darkness; he is marked for the sword ... Distress and anguish fill him with terror ... because he shakes his fist at God and vaunts himself against the Almighty. (Job 15:20–25)

Eliphaz speaks of Job as though Job were absent. He is careful to avoid naming Job, however. There seems to be in this methodology of ministry the notion that Job will take these "subtle" hints and apply what is said to himself. No wonder Job begins his speech recorded in chapter 16 with a blistering criticism of these men whom he refers to as "miserable comforters" (Job 16:1–4).

In his last speech to Job, recorded in chapter 22, Eliphaz abandons this indirect approach. He has become so angry that he takes off his gloves, and attacks his "friend" with bare fists. A whole list of very specific evil deeds Job is supposed to have committed pours from his lips. It is as if he has been biting his tongue, striving to keep these things to himself, hoping Job would come out into the open and confess them himself without the need of someone else revealing them. We may believe Eliphaz, or we may believe God and Job as they have attested the character Eliphaz so seriously attacks here:

> Is not your wickedness great? Are not your sins endless? [Note the second person singular, instead of the previously consistent third person.] You demanded security from your brothers for no reason; you stripped men of their clothing, leaving them naked. You gave no water to the weary and you withheld food from the hungry, though you were a powerful man, owning land—an honored man, living on it. And you sent widows away empty-handed and broke the strength of the fatherless. That is why snares are all around you, why sudden peril terrifies you, why it is so dark you cannot see, and why a flood of water covers you. (Job 22:5–11)

The remedy Eliphaz prescribes is a good dose of repentance, and even here he adds more accusations: Job is a miserly materialist.

> Submit to God and be at peace with him; in this way prosperity will come to you. Accept instruction from his mouth and lay up his words in your heart. If you return to the Almighty, you will be restored: If you remove wickedness far from your tent and assign your nuggets to the dust, your gold of Ophir to the rocks in the ravines, then the Almighty will be your gold, the choicest silver for you. (Job 22:21–25)

This is a very poetic sentiment. But it has no bearing on the situation of Job, who is innocent of all of these charges.

Why has Eliphaz become so accusatively unkind? Where has he gained this information about Job? Job's sufferings have lasted a long time. Can it be that the longer one suffers, the greater will be the temptation for friends to judge and condemn, the less will be the attempt to speak kindly and remain gracious? Could it be that the longer a person suffers, the greater the need for friends who are compassionate and careful about their words, and the less likely it is that this need will be met? It was so for Job. May those who know his story well not be guilty of the same callous responses that Job's friends displayed.

Like a broken record, Eliphaz ends his series of counseling sessions with Job by reiterating his view that God is not really that impressed with humanity, his creation. Notice again the high irony of his words. He does not know how important this man Job is in the great drama known as the conflict of the ages. "Can a man be of benefit to God? Can even a wise man benefit him? What pleasure would it give the Almighty if you were righteous? What would he gain if your ways were blameless?" (Job 22:2–3), he says. "Eliphaz," we want to reply, "you simply don't know what you are talking about!" Is it any wonder that Job does not even bother to respond to these last words of his friend from Tema?

The Reactions of Bildad the Shuhite

There are three speeches in the book of Job attributed to Bildad. They are found in chapters 8, 18, and 25. His last speech, consisting of only six verses, is the shortest chapter in Job.

In his first speech, Bildad wastes no time getting to the point. He refuses to beat around the bush, and as it were, shoots straight from the shoulder. He will be indirect in his accusations of Job just as the others were, but not before he states his opinion as to why Job's children were stricken. "Does God pervert justice?" he asks, "Does the Almighty pervert what is right? When your children sinned against him, he gave them over to the penalty of their sin" (Job 8:3–4). Such heartless, cruel, unkind words! According to the Prologue, the death of Job's children had nothing to do with their sin or their father's sin. They were slain in a malicious blast of satanic fury. Though obviously not immune to this supernatural disaster, they were safe spiritually because of the prayers and the sacrifices of their father.[3]

---

3. Strahan, *Book of Job*, 89, writes, "Bildad's ruthless logic, cold and keen as tempered steel, is a veritable dagger-thrust in a bereaved father's heart. It never occurs to him to institute an inquiry into the life of Job's ten sons and daughters. That is unnecessary, for their character can be inferred without more ado from their fate. God being just, they, his victims, were all sinners. After they have died a violent death, their reputation is slain with a syllogism."

Are there still grieving parents who are told that their offspring have been taken as a judgment against parents or children or both? How well I recall some close friends of my family who passed through the devastating experience of losing a baby several months old to crib death. The young parents had been attending church but had not made a strong religious commitment. The pastor came to call on them, and offered this by way of consolation: "Your baby was taken by God so that you would see your errors and take your faith more seriously." For many years that couple avoided any contact with Christianity, and for years nurtured a deep resentment against God for taking their beloved child so heartlessly. The pastor in question must have attended the seminary tutored by Bildad! Bildad's words, in the light of what we know from our reading of this book of Job, ought to make us ponder long and hard our own attitudes toward suffering, death, judgment, and the character of God. Fortunately the couple referred to returned wholeheartedly to their faith in later years, and died as earnest believers.

The remainder of chapter 8 is a predictable monologue about how the unrighteous suffer in this life. Bildad does react with words that reflect the oft-considered sentiment, "Where there is smoke [if Job is suffering], there must be fire [he is probably a worse sinner than we have imagined]." Hear his words, which translate this modern idiom into an ancient proverb: "Can papyrus grow tall where there is no marsh? Can reeds thrive without water? While still growing and uncut, they wither more quickly than grass. Such is the destiny of all who forget God; so perishes the hope of the godless" (Job 8:11–13). The implication is clear. Job is withering and dying, therefore he must be a God-forgetting, godless man. This speech, too, ought to cause us a moment's reflection on our view of divine retribution. Whenever we say, "I must have done something to deserve this," or, "That person must have some unconfessed sin in his life which has brought about this resultant sickness, or financial reverse, or accident, or family crisis," we ought to pause and listen for the echo, which may sound remarkably like the voice of Bildad.

Chapter 18 contains a verbal essay by Bildad, entitled, "This is what happens to wicked people, among whom Job is certainly a prime example." Hear his appraisal of his old friend, expressed, of course, in the third person:

> He is driven from light into darkness and is banished from the world. He has no offspring or descendants among his people, no

survivor where once he lived. Men of the west are appalled at his fate; men of the east are seized with horror. Surely such is the dwelling of an evil man; such is the place of the one who knows not God." (Job 18:18–21)

So much for Job, the man who does not know God.

Bildad has had his say. His last words in chapter 25 are brief, redundant and pathetic. How dark is his view of life! How gloomy is his attitude toward God's relations with humanity! How he misunderstands the Almighty and wrongly judges God's servant! We should pray for constant deliverance from ever possessing a spirit kindred to that of Bildad:

> How then can a man be righteous before God? How can one born of woman be pure? If even the moon is not bright and the stars are not pure in his eyes, how much less man, who is but a maggot—a son of man, who is only a worm! (Job 25:4–6)

Job speaks disparagingly of his friends' attempts at comfort many times. God himself says that they had not spoken truthfully about him (Job 42:7). I feel justified in presenting harsh comments about Bldad's ideas about the nature of humanity expressed in the above quote. Of course we must remember that the friends are all deeply frustrated with Job; he has defended himself and railed against what they believe to be their best and wisest advice to him. They, like Job can speak out of frustration and anger; they may give in to the temptation to overstate and exaggerate their case in an attempt to get their points across. Bildad may not be, indeed is probably not, summarizing the totality of his doctrine of humanity at this point. Rather, he must be understood in the context of reacting only to Job's sentiments. Even given this caveat, Bildad's words implying that Job is a maggot and a worm evoke a response of outrage.

"What is man?" asked the Psalmist, "What is man that you are mindful of him, the son of man that you care for him?" (Ps 8:4). Our answers to these questions will have to be forged on the anvil of our understanding of the Bible's definition of humanity.

Psalm 8 begins with a consideration of the heavens. The moon, the stars, the work of God's hands—how vast it is! And in comparison, what about human beings? Is humanity something puny, something meager? Not at all. Humanity was created "a little lower than the angels." There is God in his solitary deity, the angels in their majestic glory, then human beings, close to God, above all else in creation. And God's creature is wearing a crown, the crown of glory and honor. The remainder of the Psalm speaks of humanity's place of dominion and rule over all God has made. Nothing less than kings and queens of the world—this is what men and women were created to be. This is the biblical doctrine of humanity. There is nothing here of maggot or worm theology!

Of course the Bible contains the account of the fall and the subsequent depravity of God's magnificent creature. Hebrews chapter 2 quotes this psalm, and indicates that Jesus fought a great battle on earth and on the cross to redeem the world, to regain the crown, and to restore genuine human dignity to men and women who recognize his Saviorhood.

If humans are created by God, are children of God, and by grace may become sons and daughters within the family of God as the Bible teaches, how should anyone ever demean humanity or one of its representatives as Bildad does? The concept of God held by these counselors is exemplary. Their insults against humanity as stated by Bildad at least, are unacceptable and intolerable. I am grateful that Bildad ends so abruptly and does not speak again.[4]

The Reactions of Zophar the Naamathite

Job's third counselor, Zophar, also compares humans to animals in this unflattering assessment of the character of the wicked, and of course he has Job in mind when he makes this allusion: "Surely [God] recognizes deceitful men; and when he sees evil, does he not take note? But a witless man [Job, take note!] can no more become wise than a wild donkey's colt can be born a man" (Job 11:11–12).

Zophar speaks only twice in the book, (the other two friends have three speeches each), and his words are contained in chapters 11 and 20. I have already made reference to his words in the latter half of chapter 11, when I discussed the pastor who sang, "Pack up your troubles in your old kit bag and smile, smile, smile." The words of this old army song could serve as a good paraphrase of verses 13 to 20, and they are as

---

4. Strahan, *Book of Job*, 11, says, "Job's friends have a kind of fanatical belief in the greatness of God and the worthlessness of man. The former doctrine Job accepts, but his words are an eternal protest against the latter." This statement can be accepted if we remember that Job protests his innocence as God's servant, not merely defending his natural human goodness.

meaningless a ditty when sung to Job as they were when uttered by my brother clergyman in the presence of two ladies facing imminent death.

> Yet if you devote your heart to [God] and stretch out your hands to him, if you put away the sin that is in your hand and allow no evil to dwell in your tent, then you will lift up your face without shame; you will stand firm and without fear. You will surely forget your trouble, recalling it only as waters gone by. Life will be brighter than noonday, and darkness will become like morning. You will be secure, because there is hope; you will look about you and take your rest in safety. You will lie down with no one to make you afraid, and many will court your favor.

Zophar's other speech in chapter 20 is a monotonous repetition of what we have heard from Job's counselors over and over again. The wicked may think they are getting away with hidden sin, but God will bring it out into the open, and they will be grievously punished in this life. Job is to see himself revealed in these miserable hopeless words:

> What he [the wicked, i.e. Job] toiled for he must give back uneaten; he will not enjoy the profit from his trading. For he has oppressed the poor and left them destitute; he has seized houses he did not build. Surely he will have no respite from his craving; he cannot save himself by his treasure. Nothing is left to him to devour; his prosperity will not endure. In the midst of his plenty, distress will overtake him; the full force of misery will come upon him. When he has filled his belly, God will vent his burning anger against him and rain down his blows upon him . . . A fire unfanned will consume him and devour what is left in his tent. The heavens will expose his guilt; the earth will rise up against him. A flood will carry off his house, rushing waters on the day of God's wrath. Such is the fate God allots the wicked, the heritage appointed for them by God. (Job 20:18–29)

The reader may now understand why we began this book with an examination of Job's character including his own self-evaluation near the end of his speeches. That material helps us understand the grossly unfair treatment Job receives from his friends.

Again we read the accusations of oppression, greed, avarice, acquisitiveness, and selfishness leveled so unfairly against Job. The fires and floods of God's wrath are surely reserved for him.

The words of Zophar are ended. As with Eliphaz and Bildad, we wonder that friendship with Job could survive these unkind and oppressive speeches.

STUDY QUESTIONS FOR CHAPTER 5

1. In the preceding pages, readers have been urged to "ponder long and hard our attitudes toward suffering, death, judgment, and the character of God." Spend some time pondering, discussing, and making significant notes about these issues in light of our study of Job thus far.
2. This chapter might have been titled, "A Manual for Those Who Counsel Sufferers." List several insights gained for understanding and ministering to people in great pain and grief.

6

The Storms End in a Storm: The Words of Elihu and the Word of the Lord to His Servant

THE WORDS OF ELIHU: ANY NEW OR POSITIVE REACTIONS?

JOB HAS DECLARED HIS intention to maintain his integrity even if death should come upon him. With that declaration, his trial comes to an end. The enemy can no longer hope to gain anything by doing the only thing left to harm Job, that is, to take his life. Job will not be brought down as a servant of God, no, not by the worst suffering that could be inflicted upon him. No matter how fierce the storm, Job will stand with his face to the wind and will cry, "Nevertheless, I will not give in or give up, come what may!"

The storm is spent, and has roared around Job in vain. Calm can return now, and Job's vindication can be made manifest. The storm, however, ends in another storm. God is about to speak to his servant and to his servant's counselors. How will the Almighty reveal himself? God speaks from the midst of a natural rain and thunderstorm, which seems to be on the horizon as Job finishes his speeches, and which gathers momentum during the lengthy ramblings of one Elihu, who appears in the story at this point to add his uninvited opinions on Job and his trials.

> So these three men stopped answering Job, because he was righteous in his own eyes. But Elihu son of Barakel the Buzite, of the family of Ram, became very angry with Job for justifying himself rather than God. He was also angry with the three friends, because they had found no way to refute Job, and yet had condemned him. Now Elihu had waited before speaking to Job because they were older than he. But when he saw that

the three men had nothing more to say, his anger was aroused. (Job 32:1–5)

Who is Elihu, what does he have to say, and do his words add any light to Job's understanding of his heartache? The identity of this fourth counselor is a mystery. We are given no indication of his relationship to the story. We have no idea where he came from (other than the mysterious reference to the land of Ram), or how his words were received by Job, the other friends, or for that matter, by the Lord.

Elihu does not really have anything to add to what has already been offered as explanation for Job's suffering. He repeats the old ideas of suffering being instructive, retributive, corrective, and even punitive. He believes he has greater insight that his elders, but he has waited to speak until they have completed their profound analyses. When all is said and done, however, it is not clear that this young man, who so looks down upon tradition and establishment ideology, is any the wiser for his youth and his unobstructed view of the nature of things. A word to the wise youth reading Job?[1]

The opening words of Elihu's speech are almost humorous. He has been waiting so long to speak that the words pour from his lips like a torrent. Yet it takes him an incredibly long time to get to the point and say just what is on his mind. Listen to him fume and roar, without saying anything except that he has so much to say!

> I am young in years, and you are old; that is why I was fearful, not daring to tell you what I know. I thought, "Age should speak; advanced years should teach wisdom." But it is the spirit in a man, the breath of the Almighty that gives him understanding. It is not only the old who are wise, nor only the aged who understand what is right. Therefore I say: Listen to me; I too will tell you what I know. I waited while you spoke, I listened to your reasoning; while you were searching for words, I gave you my full attention. But not one of you has proved Job wrong; none of you has

---

1. Not all would agree with my negative assessment of Elihu by any means. Harrison, *Introduction to the Old Testament*, 1035, asserts, "Considerable loss can be sustained by underestimating the value of the Elihu discourses. While they may not attain to the same heights as those achieved by earlier speeches, they show considerable insight into the educational purpose of suffering (Job 36:7–11) as well as advancing the concept of an angel-mediator (Job 33:23 ff.) and making more explicit the earlier hints at a doctrine of salvation by faith (Job 33:26 ff.)." I would consider this somewhat of an overestimation of Elihu. Rohr, *Job and the Mystery of Suffering*, 149, refers to Elihu as, "clearly the comic relief before the real climax."

answered his arguments. Do not say, "We have found wisdom; let God refute him, not man." But Job has not marshaled his words against me, and I will not answer him with your arguments. They are dismayed and have no more to say; words have failed them. Must I wait, now that they are silent, now that they stand there with no reply? I too will have my say; I too will tell what I know. For I am full of words, and the spirit within me compels me; inside I am like bottled-up wine, like new wineskins ready to burst. I must speak and find relief; I must open my lips and reply. I will show partiality to no one, nor will I flatter any man; for if I were skilled in flattery, my Maker would soon take me away. (Job 32:6–22)

This whole chapter introducing Elihu and his advice is filled with nothing but bombastic verbosity. Are we to take from this that the speeches of Elihu, though introduced by himself as being so important, will probably be lacking in enlightening and enlightened substance?

The bombast continues at the beginning and at the end of chapter 33. Job's patience must wear thin waiting for Elihu to say something important. Elihu says,

> But now, Job, listen to my words; pay attention to everything I say. I am about to open my mouth; my words are on the tip of my tongue. My words come from an upright heart; my lips sincerely speak what I know. The Spirit of God has made me; the breath of the Almighty gives me life. Answer me then if you can; prepare yourself and confront me. I am just like you before God; I too have been taken from clay. No fear of me should alarm you, nor should my hand be heavy upon you. (Job 33:1–7)

And at the end of the chapter he continues:

> Pay attention, Job, and listen to me; be silent, and I will speak. If you have anything to say, answer me; speak up, for I want you to be cleared. But if not, then listen to me; be silent and I will teach you wisdom. (Job 33:31–33)

The remainder of this chapter is taken up with a discussion of the corrective value of suffering. There are times, he asserts, when God speaks to men through dreams and through night warnings against pride that might lead to perishing. Perhaps Job's experience has been such a warning, and Job had better heed it. Our pain and suffering may be a means of divine chastisement, from which a person may escape if warned, by repentant prayer. At any rate, the message is the same, "God is trying to speak to you, Job. Listen to his warnings that have come again and again through your pain. Repent, call upon God and all will be well."

Some commentators maintain that there is fresh insight in this teaching, but it would appear to be all too familiar, and, considering the story from the beginning, another incorrect analysis of Job's situation. Elihu thinks that all Job needs to do is see the light and repent. He will be like the wise man in Elihu's scenario:

> He prays to God and finds favor with him, he sees God's face and shouts for joy; he is restored by God to his righteous state. Then he comes to men and says, "I sinned, and perverted what was right, but I did not get what I deserved. He redeemed my soul from going down to the pit, and I will live to enjoy the light." God does all these things to a man—twice, even three times—to turn back his soul from the pit, that the light of life may shine on him. (Job 33:26–30)

Again in chapter 34, Elihu says nothing more than what we have heard over and over from the friends. God is just; he punishes sinners and rewards the faithful. It has always been so and always will be. As for Job, Elihu agrees with the verdict of the wise of the land:

> Men of understanding declare, wise men who hear me say to me, "Job speaks without knowledge; his words lack insight." Oh, that Job might be tested to the utmost for answering like a wicked man! To his sin he adds rebellion; scornfully he claps his hands among us and multiplies his words against God. (Job 34:34–37)

Elihu, Job has been tested to the utmost. God is about to reward his perseverance. That event, Elihu, awaits only your silence.

In chapter 35, Elihu further echoes the sentiments of the three friends: Job, you say God doesn't see, doesn't hear. In this you are correct. God does not hear or see wicked people. You think you are righteous, but you are not. The silence of God is indicative of your guilt.

> [God] does not answer when men cry out because of the arrogance of the wicked. Indeed, God does not listen to their empty plea; the Almighty pays no attention to it. How much less, then, will he listen when you [Job] say that you do not see him, that your case is before him and you must wait for him, and further, that his anger never punishes and he does not take the least notice

of wickedness. So Job opens his mouth with empty talk; without knowledge he multiplies words. (Job 35:12–16)

More could be said in summarizing Elihu's words, but perhaps it will be enough to quote what might be his conclusion regarding Job's plight:

> But if men are bound in chains, held fast by cords of affliction, [God] tells them what they have done—that they have sinned arrogantly. He makes them listen to correction and commands them to repent of their evil. If they obey and serve him, they will spend the rest of their days in prosperity and their years in contentment. But if they do not listen, they will perish by the sword and die without knowledge. The godless in heart harbor resentment; even when he fetters them, they do not cry for help. They die in their youth, among male prostitutes of the shrines. (Job 36:8–14)

It could be that the speeches of Elihu are intended to serve the dramatic function of preparing the reader for the speeches of God. One more human speaker is given his place in the center of the stage. Elihu is younger, apparently more clever, so self-assured, but really no wiser at all than those who have already addressed themselves to Job. Who is left to speak after Elihu? Only the Lord God himself after all human voices have finally become silent!

ANOTHER GREAT STORM IS COMING!

The idea that the storm out of which the Lord speaks to Job is already threatening as Job finishes his speeches, and mounts ominously through Elihu's speeches, is based on some suggestive words in chapter 26. Job speaks:

> [God] spreads out the northern skies over empty space; he suspends the earth over nothing. He wraps up the waters in his clouds, yet the clouds do not burst under their weight. He covers the face of the full moon, spreading his clouds over it. He marks out the horizon on the face of the waters for a boundary between light and darkness. The pillars of the heavens quake, aghast at his rebuke. By his power he churned up the sea; . . . And these are but the outer fringe of his works; how faint the whisper we hear of him! Who then can understand the thunder of his power? (Job 26:7–14)

Again, in the Song of Wisdom, chapter 28, Job ends his discussion of the location of wisdom with the words:

> God understands the way to it and he alone knows where it dwells, for he views the ends of the earth and sees everything under the heavens. When he established the force of the wind and measured out the waters, when he made a decree for the rain and a path for the thunderstorm, then he looked at wisdom and appraised it. (Job 28:23–27)

These words hint at the rumbling of the heavens, the occasional flash of lightning, and the first few drops of rain signaling the coming of the storm that breaks in full fury when, "the Lord answered Job out of the storm" (Job 38:1).

Toward the end of the speeches of Elihu, there is no doubt that the wind is blowing, the thunder is crashing mightily, and the lightning flashing frightfully. Elihu seems to be shouting in order to be heard as he insists on speaking over the din by which the Almighty seems to be trying to drown him out:

> God is exalted in power ... He draws up the drops of water, which distil as rain to the streams; the clouds pour down their moisture and abundant showers fall on mankind. Who can understand how he spreads out the clouds, how he thunders from his pavilion? See how he scatters his lightning about him, bathing the depths of the sea. This is the way he governs the nations and provides food in abundance. He fills his hands with lightning and commands it to strike its mark. His thunder announces the coming storm; even the cattle make known its approach. At this my heart pounds and leaps from its place. Listen! Listen to the roar of his voice, to the rumbling that comes from his mouth. He unleashes his lightning beneath the whole heaven and sends it to the ends of the earth. After that comes the sound of his roar; he thunders with his majestic voice. When his voice resounds, he holds nothing back. God's voice thunders in marvelous ways; he does great things beyond our understanding. He says to the snow, "Fall on the earth," and to the rain shower, "Be a mighty downpour." So that all men he has made may know his work, he stops every man from his labor. The animals take cover; they remain in their dens. The tempest comes out from its chamber, the cold from the driving winds. The breath of God produces ice, and the broad waters become frozen. He loads the clouds with moisture; he scatters his lightning through them ... Listen to this, Job; stop and consider

God's wonders. Do you know how God controls the clouds and makes his lightning flash? (Job 36:22, 27–37:15)

The splendor of the storm is so great that it reminds Elihu of the surpassing splendor of God. Then Elihu, too, finally gives up speaking. The voices of men are mercifully silent, and the voice of the Lord can at last be heard.

THE WORDS OF GOD TO HIS SUFFERING SERVANT

Out of the storm, the Lord God finally addresses his suffering servant. What does God have to say? Does he address the matter of the test through which Job has passed? Does he explain the reasons for Job's trial, and praise Job for passing the examination so successfully? Does he offer a satisfactory theological explanation for the prevalence of evil in the world and its mysterious involvement in the lives of even saintly people? To some readers, the answer must come as a disappointment. God does not mention Job's suffering, nor does he make any direct reference to the major problem with which this book seems to be concerned: how a good God can allow evil to exist and flourish in his creation.

However unsatisfactory we may believe God's speeches to be as far as aiding in our understanding of God, evil, and human suffering, we must remember that the Lord's words were not spoken to us, but to Job. Whatever God said, and however he said it, Job was satisfied, deeply and profoundly.

> Then Job answered the Lord: 'I am unworthy—how can I reply to you? I put my hand over my mouth. I spoke once, but I have no answer—twice but I will say no more.'" (Job 40:3–5)

> Then Job replied to the Lord: "I know that you can do all things; no plan of yours can be thwarted. You asked, 'Who is this that obscures my counsel without knowledge?' Surely I spoke of things I did not understand, things too wonderful for me to know. You said, 'Listen now, and I will speak; I will question you, and you shall answer me.' My ears had heard of you but now my eyes have seen you. Therefore I despise myself and repent in dust and ashes." (Job 42:1–6)

Job had pleaded for God to speak; finally his desire was granted, and the voice of the Almighty broke the silence. Job not only heard the voice; he saw the Lord as he listened to these speeches, and seeing he fell at the feet of the One before whom all must kneel in humility.

What did God say that so impressed his servant? A study of chapters 38 to 41 reveals the Lord delivering a lengthy lesson in natural science! In a series of challenging questions, God asks Job what he knows about creation, about the sea, about the stars, about the seasons and the weather, about the creatures great and small that make up the world of nature. The poetry is magnificent; the imagery is amazing. At first reading, however, the theological implications and possible applications are obscure and indiscernible. What has all this nature study to do with Job and the problem of evil?

Perhaps the answer will come through a patient summarizing of God's arguments. The Lord begins with a thought-provoking question, "Who is this that darkens my counsel with words without knowledge?" (Job 38:2). What a warning to all would-be God-explainers! All preachers and teachers ought to ponder these interrogative words very carefully. In our much speaking are we revealing him of whom we speak, or are we adding to the darkness of those who would learn from us?

What a profound privilege to preach the Word! What a grave responsibility to do so with care, with sensitivity, with strict adherence to the content of that which is clearly revealed in the Holy Scriptures! In the same New Testament book that mentions Job and reminds us of his perseverance (Jas 5:11), we read, "Not many of you should presume to be teachers, my brothers, because you know that we who teach will be judged more strictly" (Jas 3:1). We cannot be sure if James had God's question in mind ("Who is this that darkens my counsel with words without knowledge?"), but surely the two sets of texts stand together as a serious call to responsible proclamation, whether uttered publicly or privately.

Chapter 38: God's Control over All Natural Elements

God's first set of questions concerns creation: Job, were you there when the earth was formed, and the heavenly beings, animate and inanimate rejoiced, "while the morning stars sang together and all the angels shouted for joy?" (Job 38:7). The theological inference is: Consider carefully the truth of God's omnipotence, his existence as the Ancient of Days, and the wonderful harmony of all he has made.

God's second series of questions is: Job, what do you know of the sea and its bounds? I made it, then commanded it to stay within its boundaries. "I fixed limits for it and set its doors and bars in place, when I said, 'This far you may come and no farther; here is where your proud waves halt'" (Job 38:10-11). The inference here is that God sets limits to that which is very powerful. Even to the forces of evil he can (and does, and will), say, "Thus far and no farther!" Only God is omnipotent. Satan has power, but God has power over Satan. The devil's power is limited now, and will be destroyed altogether eventually.

The next questions are about light and darkness, day and night. God is the author of the day. He is able to call to the dawn and order her to begin the day. The dawn in turn is able to "take the earth by the edges and shake the wicked out of it" (Job 38:13). That is, the wicked, who use the night for their scheming, are shaken out of their haunts by the dawn. The inference is: Good and evil are known to God, and he is not powerless in the presence of iniquity. He can shake the world—and he will!

Then there are questions about the elements and the seasons: God asks Job if he has ever visited the "storehouses of the snow, and the storehouses of the hail," as though heaven contains great storage areas for these elements where God reserves them "for times of trouble, for days of war and battle" (Job 38:23). Does Job know how to water the earth with rain, including unpopulated areas and deserts? (Job 38:26). This latter activity may seem meaningless to people, perhaps, but God does it anyway, suggesting there are areas of his activity that are mysterious to us, hidden in the depths of his wisdom. To question God's acts is to call into question the wisdom of the Creator and Sustainer of all things. The inference here is: God knows what he is doing, and can be trusted with the governance of his creation, including humanity, and including Job!

The final questions of the chapter are about the stars, the clouds, and the rain: Job, do you know the names of the stars, and their courses in the heavens? "Can you bring forth the constellations in their seasons or lead out the Bear with its cubs? Do you know the laws of the heavens? Can you set up God's dominion over the earth?" (Job 38:32-33). "Do you send the lightening bolts on their way? Do they report to you [as they do at the call of God], "Here we are!"? (Job 38:35). Do you "have the wisdom to count the clouds?" Can you "tip over the water jars of the heavens when the dust becomes hard and the clods of earth stick together?" (Job 38:37, 38). The inference of these questions is: God can do all of this, and can be trusted to continue doing so. He is God. Whatever he does, he does as God. He knows what he is doing with nature, with humanity and with Job. The God of nature is the God of providence. As nature is in his control, so also are the lives of those who belong to him.

Chapters 39–41: All Creatures Great and Small, "The Lord God Made Them All!"

These chapters turn Job's attention from God active in inanimate creation to God the Sovereign of the animal kingdom. The lion and the lioness, the raven, the mountain goat, the deer, the bear, the wild donkey, the wild ox, the ostrich, the war horse, the hawk and the eagle: these are the subjects of chapter 39. From the smaller to the greater, from the weaker to the mightier, so God argues from his knowledge of and care for these creatures to his ability to fashion, understand and control the huge beasts of chapters 40 and 41, the behemoth and the leviathan.

God satisfies the hunger of the lion and the lioness. He feeds the ravens; he looks after the birthing and nurturing of the mountain goats; he gives freedom to the wild donkey who "laughs at the commotion in the town" (Job 39:7). It is God who superintends the untamable wild ox. It is God who created the ostrich who cannot fly, who is a very poor parent to her young, but who can outrun horses with her powerful legs (Job 39:1–18)!

The picture of the snorting, prancing, infinitely impatient warhorse at the end of chapter 39 must rank among the most descriptive pieces of poetry in the world of literature.

> Do you give the horse his strength or clothe his neck with a flowing mane? Do you make him leap like a locust, striking terror with his proud snorting? He paws fiercely, rejoicing in his strength, and charges into the fray. He laughs at fear, afraid of nothing; he does not shy away from the sword. The quiver rattles against his side, along with the flashing spear and lance. In frenzied excitement he eats up the ground; he cannot stand still when the trumpet sounds. At the blast of the trumpet, he snorts "Aha!" He catches the scent of battle from afar, the shout of commanders and the battle cry. (Job 39:19–25)

This magnificent creature is the handiwork of God, who is able to create and control the great as well as the small.

The Storms End in a Storm

The culmination of God's argument from nature is the description of two of the largest and strongest of all animals, called by the book of Job the behemoth and the leviathan. Commentators are unsure of the exact identity of these two great beasts; the hippopotamus and the crocodile have often been suggested.

The behemoth—what a monster he is! Huge limbs, swaying tail (or trunk if an elephant is understood), unafraid of anything, ranking "first among the works of God." Yet God is stronger than he; "his maker can approach him with his sword" (Job 40:19). The strongest of all creatures—but God is stronger.

The leviathan is given a lengthier description (Job 41), and again, the imagery is extremely colorful and evocative. Here is a creature not to be treated with disrespect or trifled with.

> Will he speak to you with gentle words? Will he make an agreement with you for you to take him as your slave for life? Can you make a pet of him like a bird or put him on a leash for your girls? Will traders barter for him? Will they divide him up among the merchants? Can you fill his hide with harpoons or his head with fishing spears? If you lay a hand on him, you will remember the struggle and never do it again! Any hope of subduing him is false; the mere sight of him is overpowering. No one is fierce enough to rouse him. Who then is able to stand against me? Who has a claim against me that I must pay? Everything under heaven belongs to me. (Job 41:3–11)

The remaining verses of chapter 41 are descriptive of the almost indestructible ferocity of the leviathan.

> I will not fail to speak of his limbs, his strength and his graceful form. Who can strip off his outer coat? Who would approach him with a bridle? Who dares open the doors of his mouth, ringed about with his fearsome teeth? His back has rows of shields tightly sealed together; each is so close to the next that no air can pass between. They are joined fast to one another; they cling together and cannot be parted. His snorting throws out flashes of light; his eyes are like the rays of dawn. . . . His undersides are jagged potsherds, leaving a trail in the mud like a threshing sledge. He makes the depths churn like a boiling caldron and stirs up the sea like a pot of ointment. Behind him he leaves a glistening wake; one would think the deep had white hair. Nothing on earth is his equal—a creature without fear. He looks down on all that are haughty; he is king over all that are proud. (Job 41:12–34)

With this imaginative description of the wonderful leviathan the words of God come to an end.

What has Job inferred from all of this? Have these questions about the mysteries of nature and these descriptions of the infinite care of the Almighty for the design and well-being of the smallest and the greatest of his creatures meant anything to the troubled spirit and questioning mind of God's servant?

GOD'S SPEECH: WHAT DID JOB MAKE OF IT?

The answer comes in the first verses of chapter 42: "Then Job replied to the Lord: 'I know that you can do all things; no plan of yours can be thwarted.'" God has spoken; Job is convinced by what God has said that he is unimaginably almighty, in control of all things, and that his purposes will be finally and perfectly fulfilled. Apparently he does not know about Satan; he does not know about the test; he does not know what importance there is to the divine encounter with the evil one, and the place he has had in determining the rightness or wrongness of Satan's taunting view of the destructibility of his faith and faithfulness. All Job knows is that God has spoken to him. God's words are all about the wonders of the natural world, but Job discerns that they are about divine faithfulness, divine providence, divine governance, and divine sovereignty in the realm of non-human affairs. Job can infer enough from this, evidently, to assure himself of God's faithfulness, providence, governance, and sovereignty in the realm of human living as well. Job is content to stop asking and continue listening and worshipping. He knows that he does not know all the answers, and he does not need to know them all. Some things, he confesses, are just "too wonderful for me to know" (Job 42:3). He has remained faithful to God. He is now certain God will continue always to be faithful to him. He has heard God speak, and he has seen Almighty God at work throughout his marvelous creation. This is enough for Job; God's servant is content with God's voice, and God's servant is about to receive God's reward for his endurance through desperate faith-testing trials.[2]

---

2. Of God's speech to Job, Strahan, *Book of Job*, 14, says, "One may admit that in a sense it is disappointing. It does not account for Job's afflictions, and it throws little fresh light upon the moral anomalies of the divine government of the world. It certainly does not explain the ultimate mysteries ... But it admirably serves the poet's purpose of bringing his hero back to a sane and true conception of the character of God. If it does

In his dark moments of crying out to God, Job had asked, "Where are you? Why don't you just answer me? I really believe you are there, that you are the God I have always known, the Vindicator, Redeemer, the one who knows me, knows my innocence, the one who is my friend. If you would only speak to me, I know I would be on the road to vindication and understanding."

Finally, the dreadful silence has been broken. The sufferings did not reveal God's purposes nor clarify Job's understanding; they succeeded only in deepening his distress and compounding his misery. If God had not spoken Job would have continued to question while determining to maintain innocence and integrity. But God did speak finally and powerfully, and God's mighty voice confirmed his presence, convincing Job that his trust in the God of justice and divine integrity has not been in vain. The storms through which he had passed did not strengthen Job's faith. The God who spoke in the midst of the storms confirmed that faith.

When we suffer and cannot understand why; when we pray and the skies seem to be made of brass, let us come back to Job's story and be willing to wait, and endure, and persevere. God is righteous. We continue to believe that he is infinitely good ; his sovereign purposes may allow us to be pressed beyond measure. His silence at such times does not mean that he has forsaken us; rather it reflects his confidence in us. He trusts us to trust him and to believe that his wise providential governance of our personal lives has meaning and great significance. He is there, and he will not always be silent. He trusts us to endure to the end, however long that may take, and when we do he will speak, and the promise is we will be saved!

STUDY QUESTIONS FOR CHAPTER 6

1. Find and evaluate other views of the value of Elihu and his speeches in various commentaries. Consider, for example, the suggestions made in footnote 1 above regarding Elihu. Do you find anything instructive for Job in his speeches?

---

not answer the questions raised by the inquisitive intellect, it satisfies the hungering heart. It turns Job's brooding mind from the problem of evil to the problem of good. It plies him with humbling interrogations as to his knowledge of the infinite resources of the Divine Mind. It suggests to him that He who lavishes so much thoughtfulness and kindness upon inanimate and animate nature, cares still more for man."

2. Why do you think God does not speak directly to Job's situation?

3. Discuss this chapter's interpretation of the implications contained in God's descriptions of nature, and compare them with the ideas of other interpreters. What are your conclusions?

4. Study several commentaries and compare their views on the identity of Behemoth and Leviathan. Helpful conclusions?

5. Is there any light shed on these beasts as one examines cross references to "Behemoth and Leviathan" in the Old Testament?

6. What do you think of Fyall's thesis that Leviathan is another name for Satan (see chapter 2 of this book, footnote 3)?

7

After the Storms: God's Servant Rewarded

THE STORMS ARE ALL past. The thunder is stilled, and the sky is bright, not with lightning flashes, but with sunshine and peace. Job has passed through the valley of the shadow of suffering; he has conducted himself with courage, and more importantly, like a servant of the Lord. He has come through with faith and hope intact. The last few verses of the book quickly bring the story to a happy conclusion as God rewards his faithful servant.

GOD'S RESPONSE TO JOB'S COUNSELORS

Often in these pages I have severely criticized the understanding and the advice given by Job's three friends. Justification for this criticism evolves from the Almighty's criticism of them in this epilogue.

> [God] said to Eliphaz the Temanite, "I am angry with you and your two friends, because you have not spoken of me what is right, as my servant Job has. So now take seven bulls and seven rams and go to my servant Job and sacrifice a burnt offering for yourselves. My servant Job will pray for you, and I will accept his prayer and not deal with you according to your folly. You have not spoken of me what is right, as my servant Job has." So Eliphaz the Temanite, Bildad the Shuhite and Zophar the Naamathite did what the Lord told them; and the Lord accepted Job's prayer. (Job 42:7–9)[1]

---

1. It is impossible to agree with Strahan's reasoning regarding the Lord's rebuke of the friends. Strahan, *Book of* Job, 350–51, says, "The words spoken by Yahweh in these two verses [42:7–8] can scarcely have been written by the poet. In the Dialogues the three friends are zealous for the honor of God, and their mistakes are not of a kind to convict them of the moral offence described as folly, and thereby to stir the divine wrath against them ... It seems probable, therefore, that the central part of the ancient Saga [which is of course unavailable for reference!] presented Job and his friends in another

Four times in this short passage (Job 42), God refers to Job as "my servant." This seems to be a name God delights to use in reference to Job; he used it before the storms arose, and he uses it still after the storms have abated. On the other hand, much of what the friends had to offer by way of counsel was considered "folly" by the Lord. Significantly, it is they, not Job, who are commanded to offer sacrifices as a sign they had committed sin and needed to do what they had constantly urged Job to do, that is, repent before the Lord. Job confesses his need to repent (Job 42:6); God does not respond, nor does he chastise Job for his behavior throughout the trial. That Job had spoken "without knowledge . . . of things I did not understand, things too wonderful for me to know," he himself knew to be true. That the friends had to sacrifice as s sign of their repentance indicates how serious the Lord considered their inappropriate counsel to have been. Just how careful we must be in dealing with suffering people and seeking to counsel helpfully with them is revealed in the picture of the repentant and humbled friends, kneeling before the altar fires and before Job, seeking his intercession on their behalf.

In the pages above, we have not hesitated to criticize Job's words and conclusions in discussing his reactions to his afflictions. Criticism and condemnation are not the same, however. It is one thing to disagree with Job, interacting with him on the basis of what the reader knows and what Job did not know. It is quite something else to judge Job, and consider his mistaken theologizing to be condemnable, or to assume, as his friends did, that his troubles were indicative of a sinful lifestyle. Job's troubled ravings and dark surmisings can be forgiven and at points even justified. The assumptions and judgmental conclusions of the friends were grossly unkind at best, and reprehensibly unacceptable at worst. To all of this the words of God give abundant testimony.[2] Let all who

---

light—Job bowing without a murmur to the will of Heaven, and the friends talking 'folly,' somewhat like that ascribed to Job's wife, about the ways of God. The poet finds it possible to retain the old ending of the Saga, but puts a different meaning into it." Strahan's commentary is useful most of the time, but it is amazing how much liberty he takes with the story at times, such as with this passage.

2. Strahan, *Book of Job*, 347, writes, "Job has discovered that there are questions in reference to which agnosticism is a virtue and dogmatism a sin. In his eagerness to solve the enigmas of his life, he has put forward hypotheses as if they were ascertained truths; he has charged God with injustice when he should have charged himself with ignorance; he has confidently pronounced judgment on things beyond his comprehension. But the vision of God has made him intellectually humble. He now acknowledges that things are far more wonderful than he has ever realized. Henceforth, instead of trying

counsel sufferers in God's name take note: Good intentions will not take the place of careful listening, sympathetic understanding, and humble admission of a lack of theological certitude. If these are wanting, more harm than good will result, and God will not be pleased.

JOB RESTORED AND REWARDED

Finally Job is rewarded, and thereby vindicated. His family is restored, his friends and relatives gather round to encourage him (where were they when he needed them?); his flocks and herds are double what he had before. It is a fitting end for such a noble hero of faith:

> After Job had prayed for his friends, the Lord made him prosperous again and gave him twice as much as he had before. All his brothers and sisters and everyone who had known him before came and ate with him in his house. They comforted and consoled him over all the trouble the Lord had brought upon him, and each one gave him a piece of silver and a gold ring. The Lord blessed the latter part of Job's life more than the first. He had fourteen thousand sheep, six thousand camels, a thousand yoke of oxen and a thousand donkeys. And he also had seven sons and three daughters ... Nowhere in all the land were there found women as beautiful as Job's daughters, and their father granted them an inheritance along with their brothers. After this, Job lived a hundred and forty years; he saw his children and their children to the fourth generation. And so he died, old and full of years. (Job 42:10–16)

"Does Job fear God for nothing?" Satan asked, implying that Job was good because his goodness was rewarded with God's favor and blessing. Is the Epilogue evidence for the fact that Satan was right? Do God's servants live for God in order to collect the rewards and escape trouble and sorrow either in life or in the life to come? There is no evidence in the book of Job to suggest that he served God with rewards in mind. He served his master and stayed away from what he knew to be evil because it was the right thing to do. He did believe with the friends that suffering is evidence of evil in one's life, and he knew his sufferings were in this sense undeserved. The friends remained locked into this theory, insisting on Job's guilt and demanding his repentance. Job refused to repent, con-

---

to explain all mysteries, he will recognize that it may be an act of piety towards God and of charity towards men to leave not a few of them unexplained."

vinced that somehow the theory of retributive justice universally applied in every human situation must be flawed. Through his experience we come to see that faith and faithfulness may involve God's servant in great suffering. Nevertheless, faith and faithfulness will always be rewarded. This is the teaching of the Hebrew and Christian Scriptures. For Job the rewards came in this life. For many, the rewards may be presented in heaven. Jesus said of those who persevere in the midst of great suffering, "Rejoice and be glad, because great is your reward in heaven" (Matt 5:12). The hope of the believer for a future life where wrongs will be righted and justice will be served and will everlastingly prevail is bright indeed. We live for God, not rewards. When we do, the rewards will take care of themselves.

POSTSCRIPT: THE BOOK OF JOB AND THE ANGUISHING REALITIES OF LIFE

There are many reasons why believers today may be called upon to suffer. We are not immune to the diseases and illnesses that afflict this fallen race. We may be the victims of abuse both physical and mental; we may be involved in natural disasters or tragic accidents. Our loved ones may be snatched from us by sudden, uninvited calamity. Financial reverses, occupational crises, heartbreaking family breakup—on and on we might go, listing the troubles that potentially assail even strong believers. How are we to explain the coming of these woeful visitors? Why do such storms invade the lives of those who are in God's keeping? How much of what comes to us as tragedy comes from Satan's hand, with a view to destroying us as believers? How do we counsel others, friends and acquaintances, when they are called upon to go through the fire? Where is God when the storms come?

So many questions. Many of them we will never be able to answer satisfactorily. Some of them, explicitly or implicitly, however, are the substantial heart of the book of Job. Thank God for this ancient story, for this marvelous poetry. Most of all, we express gratitude for the man Job and his sterling example of faith under fire, of faith struggling and questioning and agonizing with perplexity, and yet triumphing over all the questions and doubts and pain and storms with a triumph that brings glory to the Lord. How grateful we will ever be for the book of Job, this portrait of God's suffering servant!

After the Storms: God's Servant Rewarded

STUDY QUESTION FOR CHAPTER 7

1. Some would argue that Job ends too well, too happily-ever-after. This is unrealistic: life, it is said, is not like this. Is the ending of Job believable?

2. Does the Epilogue not contribute to the argument that if one is faithful, rewards will inevitably follow and that, therefore, God's servants work for rewards?

3. What is the significance of Job praying for his friends and giving offerings on their behalf?

4. If Job (as far as we know from the text of the Epilogue), was not told, did not know, about the Prologue, do you think that the amount of space this book gave to the first two chapters of Job was useful?

5. Briefly write a few paragraphs defending the unity of the book of Job, with reference to the usefulness of each section (Prologue, Dialogues, Epilogue) to the integrity of the whole story.

Conclusion

CORE LIFE LESSONS ARISING FROM A STUDY OF JOB

When we are seeking to understand the Bible, it is often helpful, and indeed necessary, to draw out general principles contained in any passage being considered. The next step is to consider how these truths can be applied to life in the modern world, by considering what their implications are for our lives. This is a most useful exercise when it comes to studying Job. In summarizing some of the thoughts raised in the discussions throughout this book, I have listed a number of the principles that have surfaced. I encourage you to dig deeply into this precious biblical treasure to find more and more of these living truths. Then think about their implications and applications for your life.

The following examples are far from exhausting all the "Truths for Life" to be gleaned from Job. Remember that we are striving to focus our attention only on principles contained in the text of Job. I am resisting the temptation to include other biblical truths that bear on these principles. There is some overlapping of the ideas contained in the principles. Each of these principles derives from and can be defended by reference to the book of Job.

Some Principles Are about Life in General

1. Wealth and godliness are not necessarily mutually exclusive or incompatible.
2. To hear the voice of God is faith's greatest desire.
3. We can actually please God with our faith and obedience.
4. True godliness and moral goodness always accompany one another. God is pleased with kindness, compassion, moral purity, marital fidelity, family love and loyalty, positive community involvement,

respect for others regardless of class or position, generosity, and proper reverence and worshipful fear of the all-knowing God. These traits derive from faith and characterize the person who truly walks with God.

5. God's servants are not immune to trouble or even great calamity. There are exceptions to the rule that godliness is rewarded with plenty, and iniquity with suffering. Rewards and punishments are not always meted out immediately or even necessarily in this life. Sometimes very godly people are called upon to endure very great trials, such as poverty, great personal loss, and sickness, while very wicked people live lives seemingly without trouble.

6. The suffering of godly people may be severe and long-lasting.

7. Men and women of God may be called upon to go through periods of intense suffering for reasons they may never fully understand.

8. Suffering is not always a tool used to teach lessons of life. There are times it is merely intended to destroy the faith of the person passing through it.

9. God is sovereign in the experiences of those who belong to him.

Some of the Lessons Are Precepts for Those Who Suffer

10. Patient endurance does not require that sufferers ask no questions about God and his ways. A person of great patience may also be a person who questions and even complains a great deal.

11. Sometimes the only adequate response to suffering is not to analyze it but simply to endure it.

12. Faith and endurance will be rewarded eventually.

13. There are times in the experiences of believers when unbelief and disobedience would be easier than faith and obedience. Maintaining the latter in the midst of pain and anguish is possible and, for God's child, necessary.

14. People of great faith are able to see beyond the present even when tempted to believe there is no positive future.

15. People of faith may pass through incredibly difficult circumstances and emerge with faith and integrity intact.

Other Lessons Are Precepts for Ministry to the Suffering

16. Godly sufferers desperately need the communion and companionship of sympathizing friends.

17. Those who give advice to sufferers need to be very careful. Speaking definitively for God is dangerous, because there is so much potential for harm as well as good.

18. Ministering to grief-stricken people involves far more than moralizing and demeaning them. Trivializing agony is inhumane.

19. Censuring godly sufferers is insensitive and even cruel.

20. Godly sufferers may draw incorrect conclusions about God's ways with his creatures as they raise questions and criticisms in the midst of their agony. Ministers to suffering people need to realize that suffering people may say and intimate things they would never say in less stressful times. Such sentiments must be accepted with understanding for what the individual is experiencing. Condemnation for such sentiments is out of order.

21. Listening and sympathizing are often as important as preaching and theologizing when ministering to suffering people.

Some Precepts Teach About Satan and Suffering

22. Satan possesses great destructive power, including the power to destroy human life. Satan's power is limited by God's permissive will.

23. Sometimes suffering may be permitted to demonstrate to the principalities and powers the reality and resilience of our faith and confidence in God. Can a man or woman of God endure the worst and wait for God to reveal himself? There was such a person.

24. Satan's desire is to destroy the believer's faith and confidence in God, and to destroy God's faith and confidence in his servants. God's determination is to vindicate the faith of his own children. Persevering trust in God always leads to victory.

WHEN STORMS CAME: MY STORY

The first draft of this book was written in the spring and summer of 1995. In the fall of that year, my wife Carolyn was diagnosed with breast

Conclusion

cancer. Certainly this was a major turning point in our lives. We were 55 years old and looking forward to many happy years of work and retirement together. Because of a doctor's error (her doctor admitted that mammogram reports had not been checked for the preceding three years) it was too late for milder treatment and the surgeon ordered an immediate mastectomy. "Mrs. Dow, this should not have happened. You fell through the cracks in the system, and all of your options have been used up," he told her.

Within days she was on the operating table, her breast removed and the report brought back that there was cancer remaining in the lymph nodes. They said she would be fortunate to survive the next five years. Chemotherapy was prescribed and we knew we were on the cancer trail. What I had written about storms in the book of Job was being worked out in our own experience.

For the next five years Carolyn and I decided we would make the best of life while we could. We were very much in love—sweethearts for forty years—and that love increased exponentially during that time. Her illness drew us closer together than ever. We had three great children and six terrific grandchildren, and family life over those years was deepened and broadened. We traveled extensively, to Florida, Hawaii, Israel, Alaska, and thanks to dear friends' generosity, to Barbados for an all-expense paid vacation in a luxury condo.

Then, two days before the fifth anniversary of the initial diagnosis Carolyn found another lump. We were back on the trail again, running to doctor's appointments, tests, ultrasounds, scans, labs, MRIs, and as her health quickly deteriorated, we learned all about home care, PIC lines, and pain management. More chemo, further radiation, hospitalization for tumour removal, blood clots, and bowel obstructions. Everything seemed to be going wrong at once.

Then in the autumn of 2001 a new diagnosis was given: the cancer had metastasized from the breast to the bones. It had settled in her hip and pelvic region, and became increasingly painful. More chemo, more radiation, more pain. We both knew there was only one way this was going to end. We were afraid, disheartened, exhausted, and, like Job, full of questions to which there seemed to be no answers. But like Job, we were believers, determined to follow Job's example and maintain faith in God and faithfulness to him, even as darkness deepened.

I was in my upstairs study one evening in September of 2002. I heard her cry out and a crashing sound told me she had fallen. "Are you okay?" I shouted. "No," was the feeble reply. I ran downstairs to find her on the kitchen floor. She had fallen up the stairs from the family room, and was in intense agony. I have never seen anybody in such pain. I called my physician son-in-law and he and my daughter were there in minutes. Soon, I was surrounded by the whole family and our home care worker (an angel if ever there was one), and the decision was made to call the ambulance. Off she went to emergency and a few hours later it was determined that she had a broken hip. The cancer in that area had eaten away the bone and she did not so much fall as collapse on the useless bone structure.

I was told later that many doctors would have refused to operate on a cancer patient in that condition, but we were so fortunate that an orthopedic surgeon was available who was not only willing but insisted that the hip be replaced that night. "If I don't operate within three hours, you will die of pain," was his serious assessment. The operation was successful, and within days she was home and determined to get back on her feet. Carolyn was a remarkably brave woman, and through all her trials kept a positive Christian spirit that made me love her more and more deeply.

The years 2003 and 2004 are somewhat blurred in my memory. Carolyn spent much time in bed, becoming weaker all the time. She learned to use a walker and I learned how to operate the washing machine and juggle all the household chores and shopping. By then I had retired and was grateful to be able to give her my full attention. Nurses came and went regularly, blood samples were taken often ("Is the INR alright?").

Finally the inevitable announcement: "Carolyn, there is really no more we can do for you except try and manage your pain." Doctors, nurses, chemo and radiation personnel, home care nurses and workers all loved her (who could help it, she was a sterling patient and a great human being). Many tears were shed as medical and hospital staff let her go into others' care.

For two months in late 2004 Carolyn and I left home and lived in a small apartment in a seniors' apartment complex. Meals and medical help were provided for us. I had been chaplain at the facility for some time, so knew the staff and residents well. They all loved Carolyn, and her sweet disposition and helpful attitudes made a deep impression on many there. This surely enhanced my ministry there and continues to do so as many still remember our stay among them.

In December, a few days before Christmas, Carolyn said to me, "Let's go home. I'm just too ill and tired to be anywhere else." Christmas was bittersweet; we all knew that it would be her last, so everything was done to make it special and memorable. She loved it and tried so hard to make it fun for everyone.

One bitter cold night in January, she said, "It's time, Tom. I want to go to the hospice right away." The next morning I called an ambulance, and when it drove away I said to my daughter Sue, "She'll never be back here in our home again." We wept loud and long in each other's arms together.

Her stay in hospice lasted a mere three weeks. Never once did she speak of wanting to go home. She seemed to be perfectly content to be in this, her last dwelling place on earth. Family and friends surrounded us with affection and the staff members were kind beyond words.

Pain levels increased incrementally; injection dosages grew to unbelievable levels. Finally, a lingering coma, and then, the end. Her lifeless body at last relaxed, pain free, beautiful. At her memorial service, we meditated on her joyful entry into a new life free from pain, full of joy, peace and life in the presence of Jesus.

For Carolyn, the storms were over. She was not afraid to die, and knew the Lord waited to take her home. Truly, she "endured to the end." And was saved. For me, the storms continued through months of grief and sorrow. Never could I have imagined that loss could be so painful.

Could one person cry so many tears? Loneliness, debilitating depression, confusion, bewilderment, and all the other accoutrements of bereavement threatened to smother me with heartbreak. Again, I reminded myself of Job's stubborn refusal to give up hope and something like, "if he prevailed, so can I, by God's grace," kept me going. When multitudes of questions like his came, I gave the same answers to my situation in ways similar to those I had offered him in the pages of this book.

Why did God take Carolyn from me? My answer: God did not take her life, cancer did. This insidious disease is no respecter of persons; the finest, best, and truest believers fall prey to it, and many die. This is just one of the many aspects of life in a fallen world we must accept and endure. But it is far better to be a believer in the midst of fallenness than to have no faith. Job is my evidence.

If faith is strong enough, can it not bring healing and drive out the horrible life-sucking disease? My answer: Faith in God's sustaining help is a resource that helped Carolyn and me cope with months and years of suffering. Sometimes faith brings healing to God's glory; sometimes healing is not granted, and God can be glorified through the faithfulness and perseverance of his child. So teaches Job.

Why are some healed, and not all? My answer: I don't know any more than Job knew. But when God finally spoke, even though it was not to answer Job's questions directly, it was enough to let him know that God was there and still very much God. Once God spoke, Job said he could see him with his own eyes; God's word brought an epiphany. The suffering told him nothing; the word of God lifted his head and his heart. For a long time I thought God was silent to me. I was too confused even to pray. Then I realized every thought I had was a prayer, a cry for rescue and deliverance, and as the months passed I realized answers were happening. Life was seeping back into my soul; my broken heart was being repaired as he had promised. And through his word in the Bible, he still speaks to me.

Where has she gone, my beloved? "Today," I heard him say to her, "Today you will be with me in Paradise." So she is with him now, no longer with me, no longer needing my care.

When I met Carolyn 50 or more years ago, she belonged to him. I loved her because she was so like him. My earliest memories are of prayer meetings with other high-schoolers listening to her shy petitions to the one she loved. In my imagination, I see her at spring Inter School Christian Fellowship camp, laughing and playing tricks on all of us, so full of life and laughter and mischief, so full of life and love and God. She was always true to him from start to finish. I knew I could never be other than number two in her life. That's the way we wanted it and that's the way it stayed. So finally I gave her back to her Beloved Lord. I wanted to keep her, but she was in no shape to stay. Better by far to let her go to him, healed and perfect, for eternity. We'll see each other again through different eyes and in different ways but I know I will love her and respect her forever.

Did my friends become "miserable comforters?" Did they try to say her illness was caused by sin in her life, or a lack of faith? Quite simply, some did. Did some try to pray the demon of sickness out of her. Yes. With Job, I argued (inwardly) with their theology, knowing from Job's story, this behavior was to be expected and handled. Mostly our friends were overwhelmingly kind and helpful, perhaps in part from their familiarity with and determination to avoid the attitudes of Bildad, Eliphaz, Zophar, and even Elihu.

And so the storms like those that had so buffeted Job came to us, as they do to so many. The clouds have passed for now, the rain has ceased, because, as Randall's words attest, the sun always rises. I still have days of sadness, missing Carolyn desperately. My children and grandchildren are still tender with periods of longing to have "Nan" back with us. But we are moving on. I have found a new partner who loves me and understands how to minister healing so compassionately. Lois and I have now experienced many months of happy marriage. God is so good.

> When our eyes behold through the gathering night
> The city of gold, our harbor bright,
> We shall anchor fast by the heavenly shore
> With the storms all past forevermore.
>
> —Priscilla J. Owens

ANOTHER RESPONSE

In chapter 3, I mentioned a young pastor who had just lost his first child, and the first sermon he preached after that terrible event. With his permission, I reproduce it here, because it is such a faith-filled message for those who are suffering, and reminds us that no matter how dark a situation seems, there is still hope for the future.

The Sun Always Rises

Text: Rev 21:22–27

Pastor Randall Rehkopf

Breslau (Ontario) Evangelical Missionary Church

Preached on Sunday, May 21, 1995.

Every night when we go to sleep, we go with the assurance that in the morning the sun will rise. For as long as any of us have been alive, for as long as humankind has existed, that has been true. Every time you lay your head on your pillow and drift off to sleep, regardless of where you are sleeping, you do it with the knowledge—be it conscious knowledge or unconscious—that a new day will dawn, and that the sun will rise to light the day.

There are some days, like yesterday, when we awaken to a sky in which we can't see even one cloud; there are many days when there is a mix of cloud with the appearance of the sun; and there are those days when, from morning until evening, the clouds are especially dark and especially low, and it seems as though there is no sun, no sunrise.

And you know that life can be like that. You know that there are days of sun and splendor, when the day glows like the radiance of the face of a bride, and the whole world seems to shine like the glistening of a new wedding gown in the sunlight.

And yet there are other days when any glow that might have come from any source; when any light that would normally shine from an expected source, fails to appear as it was expected. And what is seen in its place is the darkness of a veil that covers the face, not of the bride, but of the widow. And the day is covered in the darkness of the black that is worn to announce a funeral and not a wedding, so that no matter how dazzling the day, no matter how brightly the sun shines, no matter how blue the sky appears, no matter how brilliantly the flowers bloom, all of the beauty is enveloped in the shroud of darkness that permeates to the very soul, and reaches to the very center of one's being.

You know that life can be like that, when the radiance of the bride becomes the deep blackness of the widow, when the excitement of the lover becomes the misery of the spurned, when the joy of laughter becomes the grief of sorrow, when the comfort of companionship becomes the distress of sudden loneliness.

And as life's day turns to seeming night, the hopes and dreams are snuffed out; the plans and the courses are diverted; the vessels are dashed against the rocks; the crystal is shattered on the floor; the hosts of heaven are silent; and the sun seems unwilling to rise. Victory seems to be swallowed up in death; life seems to succumb to mortality; joy seems dashed by sorrow; equity seems championed by inequity; kindness seems dispossessed by cruelty; and reason subverted by chaos and senselessness.

Life can be like that. Some of us are here even this morning in the throes of uncertainty, in the pangs of despair, in the grasp of grief, in a flood of questions over personal tragedies and over the trials of others.

Conclusion

And if you aren't now, you have been at some other time, or you will be one day—for all of us experience grieving seasons of the soul that take us near to the bottom of the sea of life or toss us like a ship in a storm; and tear us like a gentle fabric that some thought was never meant to be torn; and cover us like a night that appears unbroken because of the seeming absence of the sunlight of morning.

But no matter how dark the morning, no matter how low the clouds, no matter how black the sky, no matter how heavy the rain, no matter how chilling the wind, no matter how obscured the light of the sun, it must never be forgotten, it must never be forgotten, that in the midst of it all, when each morning comes, even though veiled by the dark and hidden by the gloom, when each morning comes, the sun always rises.

When we go through a period of extended cloud and rain, when the sun does not appear for many days that are marked constantly, it seems, by dullness and dreariness, somewhere someone is certain to say: "The sun hasn't risen for days."

When life is like that, and a canopy of gloom hovers over our space, we can be inclined to make the same kind of statement—that the sun has ceased to rise, that the day no longer breaks. But whether it has to do with weather or with life, no matter the depth of despair or the length of the gloom, there is nothing that we could say that stands farther from truth, than to say that the sun hasn't risen.

For no matter the number of the clouds, the darkness of the clouds, the height of the clouds or the duration of the clouds, one thing is unchanging: The sun always rises. Never has there been a day in your existence or mine when the sun has not risen. Behind the mist, beyond the clouds, on the other side of the rain, the sun rises unrestrained, and its course remains unbroken, because the world continues on and the earth does not cease to revolve on its axis. The clouds may obscure and the fog may haze but the sun shines every day.

We may not see it. We may not be able to rise on the wings of a bird above the clouds to see the sun faithfully in its place providing even the shaded light that still guides our daytime way. We may not be able to soar above the gloom and the dread to know the sun's full brilliance and beauty above the veil. We may see it only cloaked, unrecognised because before it are many obstructions. But it still shines. It still shines.

And in those long periods of overcast days, when the sun appears to our view but briefly, or even not at all, we either scoff at it and cynically curse the day; or we can even still rejoice and be reminded, whether by its fleeting presence, or even in its prolonged absence, that it is still there, it still shines, and it will soon, in time, warm us with its heavenly rays, and teach us—if we will be taught—that it was always there, though other weather had intervened.

In truth, you know, the sun doesn't really rise. It is even more reliable than that. The sun doesn't get up every morning and then sleep at night, because when it doesn't give light on one side of the globe, it gives light on the other, and even on the first side, sending its reflection from the moon.

When we rise in the morning, we rise with the confidence that the sun's light will light the day, because the sun is always there, as this dependent globe rotates round it.

A week ago Wednesday, at 3:45 p.m., I looked west to the horizon, and saw only thick, dark clouds gathering, and sheets of rain falling in the distance. And one of the most distant thoughts to enter my thinking or my experience at the time was any thought of the sun. I felt only the building of the wind, and the chill of the air and the first drops of rain as the sheets moved eastward.

But you know, all along, without fail, dependably, reliably, faithfully, though unseen, the sun stood in its place, having risen as always, standing at the ready to be seen shining in its fullness at the break of the clouds—having shone even in the storm, providing light, even though it was dimmed.

The psalmist declared, in the 84th psalm, that God is a sun—an s-u-n. God is many things, and none of the metaphors ascribed to God will ever accurately measure Who and What He is, for God is God. But revealing Himself to our understanding, He presents Himself in many ways, showing to us His vastness, His greatness, His unlimitedness.

God is a sun, Who shines even in the midst of the gloom. God is a sun, Who, even in the darkest days, never fails to provide light for the wanderer and to show the way to the weary searcher, though the tired one may need more time to see the dim light.

God is a sun, Who has risen, and Who cannot be removed from His place of glory, whether this earth rotates on its axis or is hurled into a celestial sea or a great abyss.

Conclusion

God is a sun, Whose substance, Whose nature, Whose being, Whose brilliance, Whose power, will not change, even when life is like shifting sand.

Storms can be tracked; hurricanes can be sighted; some weather disturbances can be detected and followed; but much stormy weather occurs with little warning, little preparation, little or no understanding. Yet the sun never ceases to shine.

Life's storms can be tracked; they can be sighted; many can be detected and followed and analyzed; but many of life's storms come with little warning, little preparation, little or no understanding. Yet God is a sun, and He never ceases to shine.

Does that sound trite? It might sound trite, just as it might sound trite to say that behind the stormy weather shines the sun. If we see only the storm, the sun may seem insignificant. But if we didn't have the light of the sun in the storm, no matter how dim, we could never see through it; we could only feel it, and be swallowed up in absolute darkness and even deeper horror.

The light remains, and when we can see past the storm to the light, we see the light of hope, we see the light of the world, we see the light of life, the only light by Whom we can be saved. He shines. We may, for a time, see only the storm.

But beyond it, indeed, through it, He shines. He shines for His own to see, and He shines for the unseeing to find sight. Our storm may be the premature end of a life; it may be the near end of a life; it may be the uncertain future of a life; it may be the slow recovery of a life; it may be the stagnancy of a physical life; it may be the falling apart of parts of a life.

Yet God shines; God sends His rays of sunlight. In our storm, He has sent His Word, His Spirit, His people, and many times they have broken through the pall that has been cast, and have brought light and warmth and courage and peace and certain hope.

We will experience storms. We cannot pretend to know always why they were sent or why they were allowed, for our sphere of understanding cannot pretend to go beyond where it can. Sometimes we can know if a storm comes because of behavior or actions. But often we can't.

But we can know that though we lack explanations, we still can be taught much through the storms, after the storms, by the storms. God causes all things—good and evil, expected and unexpected, deserved and unexplained—He causes all things to work for the good of those who love Him, who have been called according to His purpose, in order to be conformed to the image of the Son.

If we go to the heavens, He is there; if we make our bed in the depths, He is there. If we rise on the wings of the dawn, if we settle on the far side of the sea, even there His hand will guide us, His right hand will hold us fast. If we say, "Surely the darkness will hide me and the light become night around me," even the darkness will not be dark to Him; the night will shine like the day, for darkness is as light to Him (Ps 139:8–12).

There's no running away. We mustn't run away. Too many of God's children run away. We must be willing and teachable as the simplest disciple, looking, even through our desperation, for the rays of sunlight offered by the Sun. And when we're not in the storm, what a thrill it is to be available as one of the Sun's rays.

There will be damage. We cannot go about denying that there will be damage from the storm that will need to be reconstructed or healed. We mustn't deny or escape the storms, or pretend they didn't happen, or bury the pain. For many, the most difficult pain to bear is not any pain of a physical nature, but the anguish of the heart, the affliction of the soul, wrought by deep and honest emotion. Some of the longest lasting wounds aren't those caused by the first grief, but those further inflicted by the lack of grief.

Will the clouds then part, and the sun be exposed, never again to be covered? We might want to say "Yes," but the rain will fall on the just and the unjust, the righteous and the unrighteous. And the sun will shine. It has to shine. He must shine.

And are there rainbows? There are those, too, in addition to the rays of the sun and the Sun Himself. But in the darkest hour, perhaps we can be comforted in the vision seen by John who saw the New Jerusalem: "I did not see a temple in the city, because the Lord God Almighty and the Lamb are its temple. The city does not need the sun or the moon to shine on it, for the glory of God gives it light, and the Lamb is its lamp. The nations will walk by its light, and the kings of the earth will bring their splendor into it. On no day will its gates ever be shut, for there will be no night there" (Rev 21:22–25). For, indeed, even throughout all eternity, the sun always rises. Amen.

I believe in the sun, even when it is not shining.
I believe in Love, even when I feel it not.
I believe in God, even when He is silent

—Unknown

STUDY QUESTION FOR THE CONCLUSION

1. Discuss the truths and precepts listed above, and add as many more as you can legitimately defend as coming from a study of Job.

Bibliography

Andersen, Francis I. *Job: An Introduction and Commentary*. TOTC. Leicester: InterVarsity, 1977.
Archer, Gleason, Jr. *A Survey of Old Testament Introduction*. Chicago: Moody, 1974.
Ballentine, Samuel E. *Job*. Macon, GA: Smyth & Helwys, 2006.
Ellison, H. L. *From Tragedy to Triumph: The Message of the Book of Job*. London: Paternoster, 1970.
Fyall, Robert S. *Now My Eyes Have Seen You: Images of Creation and Evil in the Book of Job*. Downers Grove, IL: InterVarsity, 2002.
Gibson, John C. L. *Job*. The Daily Study Bible Series. Philadelphia: Westminster, 1985.
Harrison, R. K. *Introduction to the Old Testament*. Grand Rapids: Eerdmans, 1977.
Kent, H. Harold. *Job our Contemporary*. Grand Rapids: Eerdmans, 1967.
Kushner, Harold S. *When Bad Things Happen to Good People*. New York: Schocken, 1981.
Landorf, Joyce. *Silent September*. Waco: Word Books, 1984.
Mason, Mike. *The Gospel according to Job*. Wheaton: Crossway, 1994.
Rohr, Richard. *Job and the Mystery of Suffering: Spiritual Reflections*. New York: Crossroad, 2004.
Strahan, James. *The Book of Job*. Edinburgh: T. & T. Clark, 1914.
Tabb, Mark A. *Out of the Whirlwind*. Nashville: Broadman & Holman, 2004.
Waltke, Bruce K. *An Old Testament Theology: An Exegetical, Canonical and Thematic Approach*. Grand Rapids: Zondervan, 2007.
Wood, James. *Job and the Human Situation*. London: Geoffrey Bles, 1966.

Modern Author Index

Andersen, Francis I., 1, 5, 29

Archer, Gleason, Jr., 4, 66, 79, 84, 87

Ballentine, Samuel E., 1

Ellison, H. L., 3, 29

Fyall, Robert S., 5, 29, 18

Gibson, John C. L., 29, 30

Harrison, R. K., 5, 65, 87, 106

Kent, H. Harold, 32

Kushner, Harold S., 2

Landorf, Joyce, 66

Mason, Mike, 13, 14, 30

Rohr, Richard, 2, 15, 64, 65, 94, 106

Strahan, James, 2, 7, 11, 26, 27, 31, 39, 45, 46, 73, 79, 80, 83, 87, 92, 94, 99, 102, 116, 119, 120

Tabb, Mark A., 24, 25, 65

Waltke, Bruce K., 33, 80

Wood, James, 3, 32, 76, 77, 79, 80

Scripture Index

OLD TESTAMENT

Genesis
18:25	61

Exodus
20:7	22

Nehemiah
[2:8]	64

Job
1–2	4–6, 27
1:1	13
1:4–5	16
1:6–12	28
1:8	13
1:21	38
2:1–7	28
2:2	34
2:7	29
2:8	26
2:10	24, 38
2:11–13	93
2:12, 13	26
3:3–6	42
3:20–22	70
3:26	70
3:17–19	42
3:25	43
4–5	94
4:3–4	16
4:4–6	94
4:14–19	96
5:6–7	43
5:8	95
5:17–18	95
5:19	95
6–7	71
6:2–4	72
6:8–10	72, 89
6:11–13	43
6:14	44
6:15–21	71
6:30	44
7:2–7	62
7:4	26
7:5	26
7:7	48
7:12	71
7:14	26
7:16	49
7:17–20	71
7:19	50
8	99, 100
8:3–4	99
8:11–13	100
9–10	72
9	52
9:4–10	51
9:14–24	51
9:19–20	73
9:21	89
9:24	40, 72
9:32–35	53
10:1–2	44
10:3–9	39
10:5–7	89
10:12–13	39

Job (cont.)		17:9	78
10:15–17	73	18	99, 100
10:18	68	18:18–21	101
10:20	50	18:30	26
11	102	19:2–6	78
11:1–12	102	19:6–7	57
11:13–20	102–3	19:8–12	78
12–14	73	19:13–21	61
12:2	74	19:17	26
12:7–9	74	19:20	26
12:9	3	19:21–22	78
12:13–25	54	19:23–24	78
12:14–25	74	19:25–27	79, 80, 89
13:4–5	74	20	102, 103
13:5–11	68	20:13–20	102
13:12	74	20:18–29	103
13:13–18	75, 89	21	81
13:28	74	21:4	80
14:1–2	56, 74	21:5	62
14:5–6	54	21:7–15	59
14:7–12	56	21:16	81
14:10–12	74	21:17–21	81
14:14	75, 76	22:2–3	99
14:14–17	76, 80, 89	22:5–11	98
14:18–22	56	22:21–25	98
15:2–6	96	23–24	82
15:14–16	97	23:2–9	63
15:20–25	97	23:3–7	82, 90
15:20–35	97	23:10–12	82, 90
16–17	76	23:13–15	63
16:1–4	98	23:17	82
16:2	76	24:2–7, 12	60
16:3–5	76	25	99
16:6	26	25:4–6	101
16:7	76	26–31	83
16:7–14	39	26:7–14	86, 109
16:15–16	77	27	84, 86
16:16	26	27:2–6	85, 90
16:17–21	77, 89	27:3–6	86
16:18 ff.	80	27:5	41
17:1	76	27:8–14	84

Job (cont.)

Reference	Pages
28	86, 87, 88
28:12–22	87
28:20–28	88
28:23–27	110
28:28	41
29–31	88
29	15, 17, 69, 85
29:2–6	17
29:7–17	18
29:18–20	84
30	83
30:1	84
30:9–11	84
30:15	84
30:16–19	83
30:17	26
30:20–22	83
30:27–31	62
30:27	26
30:30	26
31	17, 18, 85
31:1–4	18
31:5–6	18
31:7–8	19
31:9–12	19
31:13–15	19
31:16–23	20
31:24–28	21
31:29–30	21
31:30	21
31:31–32	22
31:33–34	23
31:35–37	23
31:38–40	23
32:1–5	106
32:6–22	107
33:1–7	107
33:23 ff.	106
33:26 ff.	106
33:26–30	108
33:31–33	107
34:34–35	108
35:12–16	109
36:7–11	106
36:8–14	109
36:22	111
36:27—37:15	111
38–41	112
38	112
38:1	110
38:2	112
38:7	112
38:10–11	113
38:13	113
38:23	113
38:26	113
38:32–33	113
38:35	113
38:37–38	113
39–41	114
39:1–18	114
39:7	114
39:19–25	114
40:3–5	111
40:4	68
40:19	115
41	115
41:3–11	115
41:12–34	115
42:1–6	111
42:3	116
42:5	68, 80
42:6	120
42:7	101
42:7–9	119
42:7–8	119
42:10–16	121

Psalms 59

Reference	Pages
8	101–2
22	66–68

Psalms (cont.)
84   134
139:8–12   136

Proverbs   9, 87, 88

Isaiah
53:6   53

Jeremiah   15

Daniel   2, 14, 18

Jonah   2, 15

NEW TESTAMENT

Matthew
5:12   122
6:9   22
13:28, 39   6
19:24–25   15
27:39–43   94

John
8:29   14
8:44   35
11:25   75
15:11   57

Acts
8:34–35   77
10:15   20

Romans
3:23   46
5:1   53
6:23   46
8:18   46
8:20–22   60

2 Corinthians
2:11   35
2:14   61
4:16–18   46
5:8   79

Ephesians
3:10–11   36
6:10–18   35

Philippians
1:23   79
4:13   44

Hebrews
1:2   53
2   102
2:10   24, 25
2:14   35
4:14–16   53
11   90
11:35–40   9
12:2   57
12:7–13   45

James
3:1   112
5:11   8, 80, 112

2 Peter
3:13   60

1 John
3:8   35
5:4   37

Revelation
12:11   35
21:22–25   136
21:22–27   131

www.ingramcontent.com/pod-product-compliance
Lightning Source LLC
Chambersburg PA
CBHW070914160426
43193CB00011B/1449